OREGON COAST BRIDGES

OREGON COAST BRIDGES

Including a Brief History of the

OREGON COAST HIGHWAY

by

Ray A. Allen

Photographs by

James B. Norman, Jr.

with a Foreword by

Dwight A. Smith

Layout and Design by

Mark A. Falby

North Left Coast Press
6327 SW Capitol Highway, Suite C PMB 111
Portland, OR 97239
© 2011 by North Left Coast Press
All rights reserved. Published 2011.
Printed in the United States of America.

ISBN: 9780983279600 (Hardcover)
ISBN: 9780983279617 (Softcover)

Library of Congress Cataloging Data

Allen, Ray A., 1940 -
    Oregon Coast Bridges / text by Ray A. Allen
    Photographs by James B. Norman, Jr. (b. 1952)
    Foreword by Dwight A. Smith,
    Design by Mark A. Falby
    First Edition
    Includes Bibliographical references and index.
    1. Bridges-Oregon-Coast. I. Title

The paper in this publication meets the minimum requirements of the American
National Standard for Information Sciences—Permanence of Paper for Printed Library
Materials, ANZI Z39.48-1984

Cover photo: Coos Bay (Conde B. McCullough) Bridge by James Norman for the Historic American
Engineering Record (HAER), 2002.

Frontispiece: Yaquina Bay Bridge at Newport, Oregon, by James Norman for HAER.

Rear cover photo: Alsea Bay Bridge at Waldport, Oregon, 1954
Wanda Gifford Collection, OSU Commons 3387225849
Courtesy of Oregon State University Archives

For Denise

Dedication

I dedicate this book to the original Alsea Bay Bridge, designed by Oregon's master bridge builder Conde B. McCullough, and to my grandparents Jesse Claire Ayers and Georgia LaPorte Ayers who introduced me to it. Its singular beauty inspired me to write a book about the Oregon coast bridges, its deterioration ignited a statewide effort to save it, and its untimely demise awakened the Oregon Department of Transportation (ODOT) to the value Oregonians place on their unique highway structures.

I also dedicate this book to Vic Sabin, proprietor of the former New World Coffee House in Eugene. He taught me the price one must pay for historic preservation. In the mid 1960s he stood alone month after month at a makeshift stand on the University of Oregon campus, often in cold and inclement weather, without pay or support, sometimes as ridiculed as respected, collecting signatures to save the old College Side Inn from destruction. In spite of his efforts, the unique Elizabethan-styled campus landmark was razed and replaced by a concrete-block building lacking any architectural merit. I never forgot the loss of that beautiful historic structure and Vic's valiant attempt to save it.

Nearly twenty years later I worked with a group of dedicated preservationists to save the original Alsea Bay Bridge, one of the Oregon coast's most cherished bridges. Like Vic, we were unsuccessful in saving that highway treasure, but just as his work helped raise awareness for preservation in Eugene, our efforts also were not in vain. The public outcry stimulated by our cause persuaded ODOT to scrap its proposed freeway-type replacement span and open a design competition that produced the distinctive arched structure that now crosses Alsea Bay. Later, ODOT insiders built a case for preserving Oregon's highway bridges, especially the McCullough treasures along the coast. Today, ODOT's Bridge Engineering Section Preservation Team seeks not only to protect Oregon's historic highway bridges but also to improve the design of new and replacement bridges.

It may be a circuitous path, but taking a stand can make a difference.

photo: Historic view of Alsea Bay Bridge, Waldport.

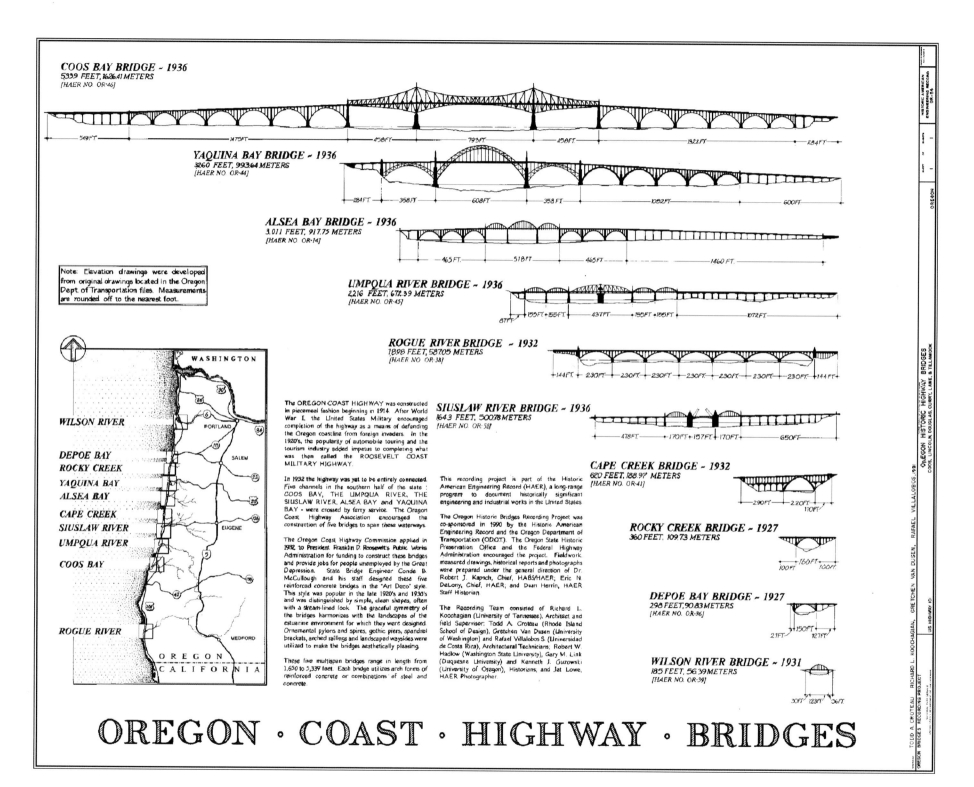

COOS BAY BRIDGE ~ 1936
5,339 FEET, 1626.41 METERS
[HAER NO. OR-46]

549 FT — 1475 FT — 458 FT — 793 FT — 458 FT — 1322 FT — 284 FT

YAQUINA BAY BRIDGE ~ 1936
3,260 FEET, 993.64 METERS
[HAER NO. OR-44]

284 FT — 358 FT — 608 FT — 358 FT — 1052 FT — 600 FT

ALSEA BAY BRIDGE ~ 1936
3,011 FEET, 917.75 METERS
[HAER NO. OR-14]

465 FT — 518 FT — 465 FT — 1460 FT

UMPQUA RIVER BRIDGE ~ 1936
2,216 FEET, 672.39 METERS
[HAER NO. OR-45]

87 FT — 155 FT + 155 FT — 437 FT — 155 FT + 155 FT — 1072 FT

ROGUE RIVER BRIDGE ~ 1932
1,898 FEET, 587.05 METERS
[HAER NO. OR-38]

144 FT + 230 FT + 230 FT + 230 FT + 230 FT + 230 FT + 230 FT + 230 FT + 144 FT

SIUSLAW RIVER BRIDGE ~ 1936
1,643 FEET, 500.78 METERS
[HAER NO. OR-58]

478 FT — 170 FT + 157 FT + 170 FT — 650 FT

CAPE CREEK BRIDGE ~ 1932
620 FEET, 188.97 METERS
[HAER NO. OR-41]

290 FT — 220 FT — 110 FT

ROCKY CREEK BRIDGE ~ 1927
360 FEET, 109.73 METERS

100 FT — 160 FT — 100 FT

DEPOE BAY BRIDGE ~ 1927
298 FEET, 90.83 METERS
[HAER NO. OR-36]

21 FT — 150 FT — 127 FT

WILSON RIVER BRIDGE ~ 1931
185 FEET, 56.39 METERS
[HAER NO. OR-39]

30 FT — 123 FT — 36 FT

Note: Elevation drawings were developed from original drawings located in the Oregon Dept. of Transportation files. Measurements are rounded off to the nearest foot.

WASHINGTON

WILSON RIVER

DEPOE BAY
ROCKY CREEK
YAQUINA BAY
ALSEA BAY

CAPE CREEK
SIUSLAW RIVER
UMPQUA RIVER

COOS BAY

ROGUE RIVER

PORTLAND
SALEM
EUGENE
MEDFORD

OREGON
CALIFORNIA

The OREGON COAST HIGHWAY was constructed in piecemeal fashion beginning in 1914. After World War I, the United States Military encouraged completion of the highway as a means of defending the Oregon coastline from foreign invaders. In the 1920's, the popularity of automobile touring and the tourism industry added impetus to completing what was then called the ROOSEVELT COAST MILITARY HIGHWAY.

In 1932 the highway was yet to be entirely connected. Five channels in the southern half of the state: COOS BAY, THE UMPQUA RIVER, THE SIUSLAW RIVER, ALSEA BAY and YAQUINA BAY - were crossed by ferry service. The Oregon Coast Highway Association encouraged the construction of five bridges to span these waterways.

The Oregon Coast Highway Commission applied in 1932 to President Franklin D. Roosevelt's Public Works Administration for funding to construct these bridges and provide jobs for people unemployed by the Great Depression. State Bridge Engineer Conde B. McCullough and his staff designed these five reinforced concrete bridges in the "Art Deco" style. This style was popular in the late 1920's and 1930's and was distinguished by simple, clean shapes, often with a stream-lined look. The graceful symmetry of the bridges harmonizes with the landscapes of the estuarine environment for which they were designed. Ornamental pylons and spires, gothic piers, spandrel brackets, arched railings and landscaped waysides were utilized to make the bridges aesthetically pleasing.

These five multispan bridges range in length from 1,650 to 5,339 feet. Each bridge utilizes arch forms of reinforced concrete or combinations of steel and concrete.

This recording project is part of the Historic American Engineering Record (HAER), a long-range program to document historically significant engineering and industrial works in the United States.

The Oregon Historic Bridges Recording Project was co-sponsored in 1990 by the Historic American Engineering Record and the Oregon Department of Transportation (ODOT). The Oregon State Historic Preservation Office and the Federal Highway Administration encouraged the project. Fieldwork, measured drawings, historical reports and photographs were prepared under the general direction of Dr. Robert J. Kapsch, Chief, HABS/HAER; Eric N. DeLony, Chief, HAER; and Dean Herrin, HAER Staff Historian.

The Recording Team consisted of Richard L. Koochagian (University of Tennessee), Architect and field Supervisor; Todd A. Croteau (Rhode Island School of Design), Gretchen Van Dusen (University of Washington) and Rafael Villalobos S. (Universidad de Costa Rica), Architectural Technicians; Robert W. Hadlow (Washington State University), Gary M. Link (Duquesne University) and Kenneth J. Guzowski (University of Oregon), Historians, and Jet Lowe, HAER Photographer.

OREGON · COAST · HIGHWAY · BRIDGES

OREGON HISTORIC HIGHWAY BRIDGES
COOS, LINCOLN, DOUGLAS, CURRY, LANE, & TILLAMOOK

TODD A. CROTEAU, RICHARD L. KOOCHAGIAN, GRETCHEN VAN DUSEN, RAFAEL VILLALOBOS, 1991
OREGON BRIDGES RECORDING PROJECT

HISTORIC AMERICAN ENGINEERING RECORD OR-54

OREGON

Table of Contents

Foreword

The Oregon Coast Highway (US 101), one of America's most scenic highways, showcases many of Oregon's most spectacular and interesting bridges. These and other Oregon bridges played an important part of my professional and personal life. High among the great rewards of my career as cultural resources specialist for the Oregon Department of Transportation (ODOT), I include contributing to Oregonians' knowledge of the rich history and variety of our highway bridges.

Many of these bridges were the creation of Conde B. McCullough, Oregon's master bridge designer. Of the hundreds of bridges McCullough designed throughout the state, many of his best reside along the coast, and these became a special interest to me. Over the years I visited and photographed many of these bridges. Also, in the summer of 1990, I had the pleasure of traveling the coast with Eric N. DeLony, then chief of the Historic American Engineering Record (HAER), photographing McCullough's bridges for a HAER project on Oregon's coastal bridges.

In the early 1980s I was fortunate to land an assignment to inventory about 1,200 Oregon highway bridges built before World War II. That project expanded into a book, *Historic Highway Bridges of Oregon* (ODOT, 1985). Under the leadership of Pieter T. Dykman, and with the talent of James B. Norman as principal photographer and design coordinator, the book became the seminal resource for Oregon's extraordinary bridge collection and the highlight of my tenure at ODOT.

A few years before we embarked on the book, our director's office referred a young man to me enthused about Oregon's coastal bridges and preserving the scenic quality of the Oregon Coast Highway. The man's name was Ray Allen. He told me that he had decided to write a book about the Oregon coast bridges, and asked for my assistance.

At the time such an idea was in its own way "historic." The only book about Oregon bridges to date was Lee Nelson's *A Century of Oregon Covered Bridges 1851-1952* (Oregon Historical Society, 1960). David Plowden, the noted American photographer, also featured five of Conde B. McCullough's coastal treasures in his fine book, *Bridges: The Spans of North America*

(Viking Press, 1974). I knew of only two other written pieces about the coastal bridges, one an article in the May 1936 edition of *The Oregon Motorist,* profiling the five major coast bridges designed by McCullough during the Great Depression, and a research paper written in 1977 by E. Shellin Atly, an architecture student at the University of Oregon. She drew from the *Motorist* article in describing the major bridges and also provided a brief biography of McCullough, including some of the innovative engineering techniques he used on the coast bridges.

Other than the major bridges, few of Oregon's coastal bridges were then even profiled by ODOT. The idea of showcasing several dozen of them in book form from border to border seemed ambitious. As an ODOT insider, I knew that it would be a difficult undertaking. Nonetheless, I thought it a terrific and timely idea. Cataloguing the bridges would provide a public record of the bridges for the first time while providing interesting historical information. It would also help promote the scenic qualities of the coast highway to both residents and tourists.

Within ODOT at the time, environmental and preservation issues began to surface about Oregon's highways, bridges, and monuments, and we cultural resource specialists were called upon to respond to them. Some of Oregon's historic highway structures, especially the McCullough-era bridges along the coast, were beginning to show signs of age. Alsea Bay Bridge especially showed a serious state of deterioration resulting from corrosion of the reinforcing bars embedded in the bridge's concrete.

Before either Allen's or ODOT's book projects had made much headway, the predicament of the Alsea Bay Bridge overwhelmed us. In 1980, ODOT announced to a local audience in Waldport that it intended to demolish the iconic bridge and replace it with a freeway-type slab bridge. This began a series of events that ultimately resulted in an organized swell of public opinion to save the Alsea, led by Ray Allen, along with Sharr Prohaska, then director of the Historic Preservation League of Oregon.

We on the inside of ODOT, especially many of us in the Environmental Section, found ourselves in a public relations vise. While we supported the efforts to save the old Alsea Bay Bridge, as ODOT employees we were obliged to support the department line that the bridge was too far gone to be saved. Compromised though we were, we attempted to walk the delicate line between the two camps, sharing information we thought relevant to the preservation group while defending the department's policies.

In the long run the old Alsea Bay Bridge was replaced, but the public outcry regarding the loss of such a treasured highway monument forced ODOT to rethink its recommendation for a replacement bridge. As a concession to the preservationists, ODOT opened a design competition that resulted in the new Alsea Bay Bridge, designed by Howard, Needles, Tammen, & Bergendoff.

The controversy also triggered profound changes within ODOT, sparking the benefits we see today in a reinvigorated and redirected Bridge Section dedicated to the preservation of Oregon's historic bridges and the construction of well-designed, site-sensitive new bridges along the coast and around the state.

I'm also happy to report that Ray's idea about promoting the scenic qualities of the Oregon Coast Highway became a reality when Sharr Prohaska and others succeeded in getting the Oregon Coast Highway designated a National Scenic Byway in 1991.

All that was many years ago. Ray's promised coast bridges book developed slowly. I know that writing any book creates challenges and takes mighty determination and perseverance. Bridge books can be especially difficult in balancing technical engineering and design issues with general public interest. Even as an ODOT employee, with all the resources available, summarizing bridge qualities succinctly became one of the most difficult tasks in writing *Historic Highway Bridges of Oregon.* For someone outside ODOT to write a book on Oregon's coastal bridges, when most of the information resided within the myriad corners of ODOT, seemed to me a monumental task.

As a testament to its difficulty, no one else stepped up to write such a book. Two recent books, however, both notably by ODOT employees, brought attention to coastal bridges and Conde B. McCullough. My good friend and colleague Robert W. Hadlow's excellent biography of McCullough, *Elegant Arches, Soaring Spans* (OSU Press, 2001),

highlights and describes McCullough's major and several smaller coastal bridges. The other, Ray Bottenberg's *Bridges of the Oregon Coast* (Arcadia Publishing, 2006), features a collection of ODOT photographs with captions describing McCullough's major coastal bridges under construction.

Yet until now no one has catalogued all the significant coastal bridges from border to border. Though late to the party, this is definitely the most comprehensive and thought-provoking book on Oregon's coastal bridges. With a personal touch it provides a current, useful, and interesting guide to forty of the most prominent and unique coastal bridges. It features bridges whose stories have never been told, like the West Beaver Creek, Drift Creek, and Coquille River Bridges. It provides comprehensive historical information about the major bridges and their sites, such as the Columbia River, Yaquina Bay, Umpqua River, and Rogue River Bridges. Finally, it tells the compelling story of the development of the Oregon Coast Highway.

This book will be an excellent traveling companion for visitors along the coast or for sofa travelers who want to enjoy the journey from their home. Either way, I know you'll enjoy the trip!

by Dwight A. Smith, former ODOT cultural resource specialist and principal author of *Historic Highway Bridges of Oregon*

Preface

I didn't realize it at the time, but Oregon's coastal bridges left an indelible imprint on me during my formative years. It would take nearly forty years and a coincidence of time and place for this to become clear to me.

It began with a sentimental journey my wife Denise and I took along the Oregon coast in the summer of 1979. Returning to Oregon after several years, we ached for a coastal getaway. Both of us had the coast in our blood. Raised on a family farm on the southern coast, Denise's coastal roots spanned a century, while I had spent many childhood summers and countless weekends at my grandparents' cabin on Heceta Beach just north of Florence. For us as a couple, the coast provided romantic getaways during our courtship ten years earlier.

From Eugene we drove to my grandparents' old cabin site. It was one of a cluster of cabins that developed around a 1930s ocean-side resort that included an auto court and general store sited adjacent to a beach access road. My grandparents bought one of the early cabins, a primitive structure even for those times, with two-by-four stud walls skip-sheathed and shingle-sided but exposed on the inside. When purchased, the oceanfront cabin sat cantilevered over the fifteen-foot bank above the beach, where it had landed after being picked up by a high wave during a ferocious winter storm.

My grandparents paid $1,500 for the cabin, not including moving it back to its proper site.

Hecata (Heceta) Beach Resort,

Originally purchased as a vacation retreat, in the mid 1940s it became their primary residence after my grandfather suffered a heart attack. Then in their sixties, they lived there for more than a decade, the first few years without indoor plumbing or electricity. These were the years of my youth, and it became my favorite place in the world.

I hadn't visited the site in many years, and the changes I found that day hit me hard. Some of the cabins remained, but the auto court had vanished, along with my grandparents'

cabin. Only the garage remained, a leaning weathered relic overwhelmed by salal bushes and blackberry briars. Where the auto court once stood, a huge condominium complex now loomed only a stone's throw away.

I walked to a little knoll on the edge of the bank, a favorite ocean lookout where my sisters and I often played and, in season, picked wild strawberries. Along with a couple of cabins, the knoll remained the last separation from the condominiums. Standing there, the beach and surf in view, I could see the old cabin in

Shingle-sided cabin of Ray Allen's grandparents at Heceta Beach.

its beauty. Stopping the car to get a better look, Denise and I marveled at the structure's interplay of arches above and below the highway deck, and how comfortably it fit into its surroundings. Seeing the bridge again awakened more memories.

I recalled that the Alsea Bay Bridge, while not a short drive, often became the destination of many of those childhood automobile trips with my grandparents. My grandmother, always trying to accommodate her restless grandchildren, her retired and recalcitrant

Ray Allen at Heceta Beach cabin.

my mind's eye, and my childhood memories of the wonderful times I spent there flooded over me. Then my reverie ended, and for the first time since my grandparents sold my much-beloved cabin, I felt an unexpected sense of relief. Nothing that remained at the site had any meaning for me now. I remember telling Denise that I was glad I didn't have to go back there anymore.

We left the cabin site and drove north over Heceta Head, whose iconic lighthouse lingered

as one of my earliest memories. Along the way we crossed Cape Creek Bridge, still reigning over a favorite beach and picnic spot, past the touristy Sea Lion Caves, then on to Cape Perpetua, Yachats, and Waldport. Driving this unusually scenic route revived memories of many similar trips I had taken as a child with my grandparents and sisters.

Then, as we reached Waldport, the old Alsea Bay Bridge appeared. I hadn't seen the bridge in many years and was literally stunned by

The original Alsea Bay Bridge at Waldport.

engineer husband, and her own passion for outings, often found common ground by promoting picnic trips to "the bridge." Having designed some modest dams and bridges himself, my grandfather loved the Alsea Bay Bridge. Since only he could drive, indulging him was important. While Heceta Head and its beach below Cape Creek Bridge often entertained us, the Alsea became his—and our—most treasured destination.

As those long-dormant memories swept over me that day, something stirred. I turned the car around and backtracked to find some good sites for photographs. By chance we stopped across from an old abandoned gas station, an interesting site in itself. Camera in hand, I began framing some shots for the gas station when an elderly woman came out of an adjacent house, curious as to what we were doing. Explaining our interest in the bridge, she told us that she and her carpenter husband moved to the coast during the Great Depression so that he could work on the bridge. She had lived there ever since.

After chatting with her and taking photos of the bridge, we headed on up the coast, continuing to talk about the bridge and the woman's story. It occurred to me that there were a lot of other impressive bridges along the Oregon coast, and that visitors like us would be interested in them

and their stories. Why not write a book about them? With a few free weeks on our hands, Denise and I began driving to Salem to research the bridges, and the basic concept for a book began to emerge. Then, as often happens, unexpected events intervened and the book project was shelved for a time, though not forgotten.

Following that trip up the coast in 1979, we bought a beach cabin north of Depoe Bay on Lincoln Beach, by chance an updated version of my grandparents' cabin. This became our primary residence until we settled in Portland in 1982. During that period I commuted between Oregon and Idaho, where we still had business interests. In early 1980, Denise heard rumors that the Oregon Department of Transportation (ODOT) planned to demolish the old Alsea Bay Bridge and replace it with a freeway slab-type bridge. I was out of state, but Denise attended early ODOT briefings in Waldport that confirmed the rumors. She became an original member of the "Save Our Bridge" committee, a local preservation group created by Waldport pharmacist Joe Bird.

It was obvious to us this was not just a local issue, but word was slow to get out to Oregonians around the state, so when we moved to Portland in 1982, I contacted Sharr Prohaska, director of the Historic Preservation League of Oregon. Together with other preservationists, we led a statewide effort to save the old Alsea Bay Bridge. Around this time our second son Cooper was born, and I started a new job. There was little time for the bridge book. Nonetheless, I continued to work on the book as best I could, alone.

Not long after, *Historic Highway Bridges of Oregon* was published. Dwight Smith, its principal author and an early supporter of my bridge book idea, opened many doors for me at ODOT. The first noteworthy book on Oregon's bridges since Lee Nelson's *A Century of Oregon Covered Bridges 1851-1952, Historic Highway Bridges of Oregon* catalogued Oregon's historic bridges, including many bridges along the Oregon coast. Familiar with my coastal bridges book project, Dwight was kind enough to inquire whether the publication of their book might in some way undermine my efforts. I assured him that I thought their book would bring much-needed attention to Oregon's bridges, including those along the coast. Since my book focused only on the coastal bridges and would provide more comprehensive bridge and historical information on the bridges profiled, it would stand on its own. Nonetheless, I was frustrated. My idea to write a book about the Oregon coast bridges predated *Historic Highway Bridges of Oregon* by five years, but my efforts at that point fell far short of a book.

Then, in 1989, Sharon Wood published *The Portland Bridge Book* (Oregon Historical Society, 1989). I remember reading her bridge series in *The Oregonian* and thinking that she should turn the articles into a book, and so she did. I saw that there would be a joint dedication of Wood's and ODOT's bridge books at the Hawthorne Bridge in Portland. I wanted to attend the event, but in the end I couldn't do it. In my mind there should have been a trio of bridge books—ODOT's, Wood's, and mine.

Still, it's an ill wind that doesn't blow some good. That event reinvigorated my efforts to finish my book. Not long after, I completed a draft that was reviewed by several people, including Dwight Smith, who encouraged me to finalize it and find a publisher. I decided to add a chapter on the development of the Oregon Coast Highway, an idea encouraged by a publisher who was interested in the book. Researching and writing that chapter took several more years and virtually became a book in itself. While interesting in its own right, I have included only an abbreviated version here. As I write this *Preface,* that was nearly ten years ago. Some things, it seems, just take a long time to finish.

Introduction

Along the more than three hundred fifty miles of Oregon's coastline runs one of the world's most scenic routes, US 101, commonly known as the Oregon Coast Highway. Along its path this extraordinary roadway travels through a diverse and challenging series of geologic treasures. It crests and cuts through giant fists of rocky headlands whose promontories showcase spectacular ocean vistas. It crosses great rivers that meander through long, broad valleys thick with alluvial soil, backed by dense evergreen forests; it passes bright glassy bays and estuaries created by the relentless run of rivers against the eternal ebb and flow of the tides, and traces broad dark pancakes of tidal flats sporting long low reaches of grassy marshes. It skirts shimmering lakes laced by forests of knotted pine and slender fir buttressed by rolling windswept sand dunes, and runs down southern coastal plateaus stationed like flatirons along the ocean's edge. And most beckoning of all, US 101 tracks the 350-mile continental hem of spectacular sandy beaches, Oregon's most treasured destination, virtually all of them open forever for public use.

Traveling this route one encounters an astonishing variety of rivers and waterways, a by-product of Oregon's legendary rainfall and consequent runoff that surges down from the Oregon Coast Range, the Cascades, and beyond. Here flows one of this country's premier rivers, the majestic Columbia that once held promise as the fabled Northwest Passage. Other major rivers such as the Siuslaw, Umpqua, Coquille, and Rogue (whose names reflect our Native American heritage) became early transportation routes between the inland valleys and the coast. Lesser but equally historic rivers such as the Wilson, Siletz, Kilchis, Nehalem, and Winchuck, along whose banks communities, businesses, and recreational enterprises developed, wind their way to the coast. Finally, big beautiful bays such as Youngs, Nehalem, Yaquina, Alsea, and Coos, along with hundreds of creeks, sloughs, gullies, and ditches dot the length of the Oregon coast, bearing the names of known and unknown people, landmarks, and meanings. These bountiful and diverse waterways combine to create a magically-stitched aqueous patchwork quilt that spreads its own distinctive imprint on the coast's extraordinary landscape.

In order to construct the Oregon Coast Highway we enjoy today, all these waterways had to be crossed, which finally meant the construction of bridges—as many bridges as there are waterways. According to the Oregon Department of Transportation *2011 Bridge Log*, there are more than 450 bridges along the Oregon Coast Highway. That's about one every three-quarters of a mile!

These bridges vary from simple drainage culverts hardly noticeable from the highway to some of the largest and most spectacular human-made bridges in the United States. Of the three major bridge types: beam, arch, and suspension, only the suspension bridge is not represented along the coast highway.

This book profiles forty of the most notable of these bridges, including the biggest, longest, highest, oldest, newest, most unusual, most interesting, and even the worst. They are highlighted by some of the best designs of Conde B. McCullough, Oregon's master bridge designer and bridge engineer for the Oregon State Highway Department (now the Oregon Department of Transportation (ODOT)) from 1919 until

Cooks Chasm Bridge is one of over 450 bridges along the Oregon Coast Highway.

1

1937. His specialty was the concrete arch, and many of his finest efforts are showcased along the highway. American photographer David Plowden's splendid book *Bridges: The Spans of North America* (Viking, 1974) describes McCullough's coastal spans as "the most interesting concentration of concrete bridges in America." Indeed, McCullough's masterpieces are so prominently displayed that the coast highway has truly become a "motoring museum" of his work.

Bridges now span the eight major waterways along the Oregon coast. From north to south they include: Columbia River, Youngs Bay, Yaquina Bay, Alsea Bay, Siuslaw River, Smith/Umpqua Rivers, Coos Bay, and Rogue River. These bridges are sometimes referred to as "major bridges," a title that reflects size rather than quality, although the latter is not in dispute. Other than the Columbia River Bridge, Youngs Bay Bridge and the new Alsea Bay Bridge that replaced a McCullough bridge, Conde McCullough designed all the other major spans. Many of his smaller masterpieces are also included, such as Old Youngs Bay Bridge, Lewis and Clark River Bridge, Wilson River Bridge, Depoe Bay Bridge, Rocky Creek Bridge, Cape Creek Bridge, Cummins Creek Bridge, Tenmile Creek Bridge, and Big Creek Bridge. In fact, more than a third the bridges profiled in this book were either designed or influenced by McCullough, and constructed during an enormously productive fifteen-year period between 1921 and 1936.

With the following exceptions, all of the bridges in this book are on US 101: Old Youngs Bay and Lewis and Clark River

Highway 101 at Neahkahnie Mountain.

Bridges, unique McCullough movable spans, sit on Oregon 105, originally US 101. Because of its singular style and proximity to US 101, Necanicum River (Seaside) Bridge on Broadway St. in Seaside is listed. Drift Creek Bridge, the only covered bridge in this collection, began its life on an early route of the Oregon Coast Highway. It now sits off US 101, but how it got there is a story worth telling. Rocky Creek Bridge made the list because it is one of McCullough's early smaller classic bridges and serves as the northern entry to Otter Crest Loop, also part of the original Oregon Coast Highway. To the south Euchre Creek Bridge on Ophir County Road is included since it is an early McCullough beam bridge that sat on an early route of US 101, and is less than a mile off the current highway.

For most observers, a bridge's superstructure captures the imagination. Others, however, are fascinated by the often hidden supports and technical aspects of bridge construction, such as unseen piling and piers upon which the bridges stand, the cofferdams and drilling rigs used in their construction, and other esoteric construction techniques. To accommodate these interests,

I have provided some of this information when it was either interesting or important to a particular structure, such as the use of the Freyssinet technique employed in the concrete arches of the Rogue River Bridge. In the interest of general appeal and brevity, I did not include detailed descriptions of bridge foundations and structural complexities. For those who are interested, I offer some resources in Appendix 3, titled Bridge Construction Techniques.

Most of the technical information about the bridges comes from the *2011 Bridge Log*. I have also drawn from *Historic Highway Bridges of Oregon* for some structural and architectural bridge details. Robert Hadlow's *Elegant Arches, Soaring Spans* has been helpful in describing McCullough's techniques regarding his tied-arch bridges, his use of the Armand Considère hinge, and Eugène Freyssinet's method of precompression for reinforced-concrete bridges.

For some reason, ODOT and other sources do not use a possessive apostrophe for most bridges and waterways along the coast. In the interest of consistency, I have deleted apostrophes on the bridges and related waterways.

Finally, I took liberties in critiquing some of the bridges profiled here. I hope it's obvious that my intent is not to demean anyone's design or work, but rather to point out what McCullough's legacy has taught us: Thoughtfully designed bridges sensitive to the surrounding environment provide a smoother, quicker coastal tour, and enhance the panoramic beauty of the Oregon Coast Highway. I found they offer a journey rich in Oregon's coastal history as well.

The Bridges

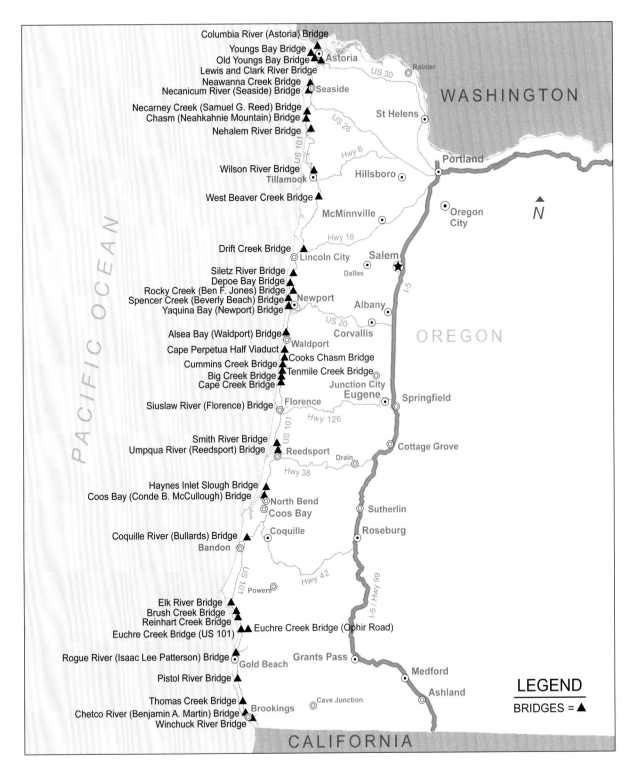

Columbia River (Astoria) Bridge
Youngs Bay Bridge
Old Youngs Bay Bridge
Lewis and Clark River Bridge
Neawanna Creek Bridge
Necanicum River (Seaside) Bridge
Necarney Creek (Samuel G. Reed) Bridge
Chasm (Neahkahnie Mountain) Bridge
Nehalem River Bridge

Wilson River Bridge

West Beaver Creek Bridge

Drift Creek Bridge

Siletz River Bridge
Depoe Bay Bridge
Rocky Creek (Ben F. Jones) Bridge
Spencer Creek (Beverly Beach) Bridge
Yaquina Bay (Newport) Bridge

Alsea Bay (Waldport) Bridge
Cape Perpetua Half Viaduct
Cooks Chasm Bridge
Cummins Creek Bridge
Tenmile Creek Bridge
Big Creek Bridge
Cape Creek Bridge

Siuslaw River (Florence) Bridge

Smith River Bridge
Umpqua River (Reedsport) Bridge

Haynes Inlet Slough Bridge
Coos Bay (Conde B. McCullough) Bridge

Coquille River (Bullards) Bridge

Elk River Bridge
Brush Creek Bridge
Reinhart Creek Bridge
Euchre Creek Bridge (US 101)
Euchre Creek Bridge (Ophir Road)

Rogue River (Isaac Lee Patterson) Bridge

Pistol River Bridge

Thomas Creek Bridge
Chetco River (Benjamin A. Martin) Bridge
Winchuck River Bridge

WASHINGTON
Rainier
Astoria
US 30
St Helens
Seaside
US 26
Hwy 6
Portland
Tillamook
Hillsboro
McMinnville
Oregon City
N
Hwy 18
Salem
Lincoln City
Dallas
Newport
Albany
I-5
Corvallis
OREGON
US 20
Waldport
Junction City
Eugene
Springfield
Florence
US 101
Hwy 126
Reedsport
Cottage Grove
Drain
Hwy 38
North Bend
Coos Bay
Sutherlin
Coquille
Roseburg
Bandon
US 101
Powers
Hwy 42
I-5 / Hwy 99
Gold Beach
Grants Pass
Medford
Ashland
Cave Junction
Brookings
CALIFORNIA
PACIFIC OCEAN

LEGEND
BRIDGES = ▲

Map of bridge sites along Oregon Coast Highway.

3

The Columbia River Bridge in Astoria extends over four miles, providing an important connection between the states of Oregon and Washington.

Columbia River (Astoria) Bridge

COLOSSUS OF THE COLUMBIA

At the completion of the original Oregon Coast Highway in 1932, only the Rogue River Bridge crossed a major waterway along the Oregon coast. By 1936, thanks to the Oregon Coast Bridges Project[1], bridges crossed all of Oregon's major coastal waterways save the mighty Columbia River. For the next quarter century it remained the lone obstacle in completing the long-sought dream of a Trans American Highway—a continuous, uninterrupted motor route between the Canadian and Mexican borders. In 1964, a new Youngs Bay Bridge provided a more direct connection into Astoria, bypassing the older Lewis and Clark River and old Youngs Bay Bridges. Only a Columbia River span remained—the ultimate challenge for regional transportation planners.

By far the longest bridge on the Oregon Coast Highway, the Columbia River Bridge, sometimes known as the Astoria or Astoria-Megler Bridge, required a decade of planning and four years to build. At just over four miles long, it quadruples the length of its nearest coastal rival, the Coos Bay Bridge, and surpasses the length of the seven next-longest Oregon coast bridges combined. Its massive 2,468-foot main truss stretches nearly a third longer and 100 feet higher than the 1,708-foot truss of the Coos Bay Bridge.

The price tag came in large too. On April 27, 1961, Governor Mark O. Hatfield put his signature on Oregon House Bill 1457 authorizing the sale of $24 million in bonds for the construction of the bridge, a cost virtually equaling that of the entire Oregon Coast Highway.[2] That September, the Oregon and Washington State Highway Commissions entered into an agreement to construct the bridge. In the fifty-five years between the completion of the Oregon Coast Bridges Project in 1936 and the new Alsea Bay Bridge in 1991, Youngs Bay Bridge and the Columbia River Bridge were the only major spans built along the coast.

The Columbia River span ended the last operating ferry service along the Oregon Coast Highway. The use of ferries at the mouth of the Columbia River began in 1840 when Solomon Smith, Astoria's first schoolteacher, lashed two canoes together and carried passengers and cargo across the river.[3] Ferries intermittently served the area into the beginning of the twentieth century. When the Columbia River Highway (US 30) opened a direct overland link between Portland and Astoria in 1915, automobile traffic through Astoria rose, creating pressure for more dependable ferry service. Seeing opportunity, Captain Fritz Elfving established the first commercial auto ferry service in 1921, when the *Tourist I* made her maiden voyage. For forty years ferries kept the traffic moving, but there were some drawbacks. For one thing, they were slow. In good weather the 4.5-mile trip took half an hour. Since the boats could hold only a limited number of vehicles, motorists often endured long waits in heavy traffic. And in bad weather, a frequent occurrence during the winter, the ferries often didn't run at all, forcing traffic to use the Longview Bridge fifty miles upriver. In 1946, to enhance the ferry service, the State of Oregon purchased Elfving's

COLUMBIA RIVER BRIDGE
Technical Data

Location: Astoria, Clatsop County (Oregon) and Megler vicinity, Pacific County (Washington); Oregon Coast Highway (US 101), Milepost 0.00

Year completed: 1966

Type: Steel through truss (cantilever); at the time of construction, it was thought to be the longest continuous steel truss series in the world.

Length: 4.1 miles (21,677 feet) (2011 *Bridge Log*)

Deck to streambed: 260 feet

Description: The main span of the structure is a 2,468-foot steel cantilever through truss made up of two 618-foot outer truss sections and a 1,232-foot central truss span. The cantilever truss is flanked by five steel deck trusses, 140 eighty-foot concrete deck girder spans and, at the Washington end of the bridge, seven 350-foot steel through truss spans. The bridge design was a joint effort of the state highway departments of Oregon and Washington.

Bridge engineer: Ivan D. Merchant

Cost: $24,000,000

Ownership: State of Oregon and State of Washington

company and assigned operational control to the Oregon State Highway Department, now Oregon Department of Transportation (ODOT).

Spanning the mouth of the mighty Columbia River challenged modern engineers much like discovering the "River of the West" tested mariners of an earlier age. Spaniard Bruno de Hezeta (Heceta) usually gets credit for first sighting the Columbia River in 1775. British explorer James Cook, who first sighted and named Cape Foulweather near Yaquina Bay, somehow missed the great river as he battled storms on his journey up the coast in 1778. In the spring of 1792, British Captain George Vancouver noted the Columbia's colorful effluence yet did not pursue its source. A few weeks later, American Captain Robert Gray, sailing out of Boston in his ship *Columbia Rediviva* ("Columbia Reborn"), first crossed the Columbia bar on May 11, 1792. He named the great river after the worthy ship that brought him there.[4]

The idea of bridging the broad mouth of the Columbia River certainly would have been beyond the vision of men like Gray and the intrepid Lewis and Clark, whose historic trek reached the Columbia's terminus only thirteen years later in 1805. In fact, it would take another hundred years and a revolution of industry before such a fantastic idea would be conceived. No one knows who first envisioned bridging the Columbia at Astoria. There is no record of such a bridge being contemplated when the idea for an Oregon Coast Highway evolved during the early years of the twentieth century. We do know, however, that in 1928, E.M. Elliott and Associates of Chicago proposed building a bridge across the Columbia at Astoria.[5] By 1930, upriver at Longview, the Columbia River was crossed by another cantilever designed by Joseph Strauss, who later earned fame as the designer of the San Francisco Golden Gate Bridge. According to ODOT, a bridge at Astoria was strongly promoted during the 1930s as a Public Works Administration project.[6] Locally, officials attempted to find money three times—in 1932, 1941, and 1944.[7] By 1944, McCullough and others reviewed various options for crossing the Columbia River below Longview, including a suspension bridge, but finally concluded that such a bridge might be vulnerable to military attack.[8] Prior to the completion of the original Oregon Coast Highway in 1932, however, bridging the Columbia at its mouth was at best an engineering fantasy.

Once the Oregon Coast Highway was completed, civic leaders and transportation officials in Oregon and Washington began repeated

Grandstand for Columbia River Bridge opening ceremony.

attempts to generate interest and funding to bridge the mouth of the Columbia. Finally in 1953 the Port of Astoria formed a partnership with the Oregon State Highway Department, the Washington Toll Bridge Authority, and Pacific County, Washington, to assess the feasibility for building such a span. In 1957

the Oregon and Washington legislatures appropriated $100,000 to prepare plans, and in 1961 they agreed to fund the project as a joint venture.[9]

On August 9, 1962, Oregon Governor Hatfield, employing a gold shovel, turned

the first dirt along the riverbank in Astoria. This act officially commenced the project, although actual construction didn't begin until November 5. The concrete foundation piers were cast at nearby Tongue Point, just four miles upriver from the bridge site. The steel superstructure components, built in sections

The bridge as it appeared during its construction in the mid-1960s.

The bridge as it appears today.

ninety miles upriver in Vancouver, were then barged to the construction site and boosted in place by giant hydraulic jacks. From start to finish, the job took 1,356 days and consumed gigantic amounts of material: 158,785 linear feet of steel piling; 134,090 linear feet of timber piling; 76,496 linear feet of prestressed-concrete piling; 97,995 cubic yards of concrete; 6,005 tons of steel reinforcing bar; 12,500 tons of structural steel; 25,290 linear feet of aluminum parapet rail; and 440,000 board feet of treated lumber.[10]

One of the largest cantilever bridges in the world, Astoria's main span reaches an impressive 1,232 feet in length, yet it is actually shorter than the tied-arch central span of the Fremont Bridge in Portland that measures in at 1,255 feet. Designers created the bridge to withstand a harsh coastal environment of high winds, fierce winter storms, and river floods. Prestressed-concrete beam spans, set on massive concrete piers and located so as not to overload the slide-prone Astoria Hills, were designed to take on flood debris—even whole trees that often rush down the swollen waters of the Columbia.[11]

Although successful from a utilitarian point of view, aesthetically the bridge proves difficult to assess. Since the river's shipping channel runs close to the south bank, the southern approach of the main span lands high up on the bank, somewhat overpowering the western end of Astoria and making the bridge appear out of balance. Lacking adequate room for a more conventional ramp approach, the southern connector twists into an awkward 360-degree, counterclockwise corkscrew that rises nearly 200 feet. Also, the long series of

Central spans of the Columbia River Bridge looking north.

View of the bridge trusses as the bridge makes connection with the state of Washington.

Times coined it the "Bridge to Nowhere," which became its long-time epithet. Others predicted that toll receipts would never pay off the huge cost of the bridge. Tolls ranged from $1.50 for cars to $4 for large truck-trailers. Early on, when toll collections failed to meet bond obligations, annual deficits often rose into the million-dollar range. Because of the initial agreement between Oregon and Washington, Oregon shouldered approximately 80 percent of the deficit, which it paid off through gas tax funds.[13]

Over time, bridge critics were proven wrong. As a connector between the lonely but appealing coastal corners of northwest Oregon and southwest Washington, the bridge began to attract visitors. While the bridge didn't create the economic boom that some of its backers had predicted, civic leaders on both sides of the river agreed that the bridge helped grow business. Jean Hallaux, manager of the Astoria Chamber of Commerce when the bridge opened, believed that the bridge improved commerce more than it did tourism in Astoria. In his words, "There's a lot of things that can go across the bridge that couldn't go across the ferries."[14]

One of the last ferry runs before the opening of the Columbia River Bridge.

trestles, accounting for most of the bridge's length, is commonplace, as are the steel through truss spans that connects the bridge to the Washington mainland. Still, its great size, various bridge types, and overall length combine to make it a very impressive span.

On August 27, 1966, four years and two weeks after Governor Hatfield officially commenced the project with his shovelful of dirt, he and Washington's governor Daniel Evans, ably

assisted by Miss Oregon Estrellita Schid and Miss Washington Sandra Lee Marth, cut the ribbon that formally opened the bridge. More than 30,000 people attended the dedication ceremonies, including some who were transported from Portland on a special train provided by the Spokane, Portland, and Seattle Railway.[12]

Widely hailed as an engineering triumph, the bridge also had its detractors. The *Los Angeles*

During its opening year, 206,216 vehicles crossed the bridge. By 1993, the annual crossings had risen to more 1.6 million, allowing the bonds to be paid off and the tolls eliminated two years early. Today, about 6,000 vehicles a day cross the Columbia River Bridge, and US 101 remains unbroken between the Canadian and Mexican borders. The "Bridge to Nowhere" has become Astoria's—and Oregon's—"Bridge to the World."[15]

Youngs Bay Bridge is one of only two vertical lift bridges on the Oregon Coast.

NEW YOUNGS – OLD TECH

The Rodney Dangerfield of Oregon Coast bridges, Youngs Bay gets no respect. Third longest of the coast bridges, exceeded only by the Columbia River and Coos Bay Bridges, its undistinguished long approach trestles and the central span's utilitarian design make it easy to ignore as one of the major coast bridges. Nonetheless, its connection to Astoria, the north coast's largest town, and the traffic volume moving both over and under it make it one of the coast's busiest and most important spans.

Constructed in 1964, its only pretense to stature and beauty likely ended with its opening, when on a chilly rainy day in August, Wayne Nunn, executive assistant to and stand-in for Governor Mark O. Hatfield, along with the glamorous Carol Pederson, that year's Miss Oregon, jointly cut a red ribbon to officially open the bridge.[1]

The bridge may be undistinguished, but interesting nonetheless. One of only two vertical lift bridges on the coast (the Coquille River Bridge is the other), the central lift span is a 153-foot steel pony truss with a vertical clearance of seventy-nine feet when in raised position. The 300,000-pound center span is lifted by four 40-horsepower electric motors, with more than a little help from the dual 266-ton concrete counterweights suspended in steel towers at each end of the span. The raising of this gigantic center span once or twice a day to allow boats to pass below creates an entirely different kind of bridge opening.

In contrast to the stately and ceremonial original opening, these explosive opening events produce mechanized pandemonium. Ready for the moment, bridge tenders monitor approaching watercraft. Suddenly sirens wail, warning lights flash, and barriers lower to stop traffic on the bridge as the center span rises, allowing water traffic to pass beneath. For

motorists and others crossing the bridge, these openings provide a few minutes to either stretch or stress, but a memorable moment either way.

For the draw bridge tender crew that works all the bridges around Astoria, these openings require a quick response. At one time, fourteen tenders worked three shifts to cover a 24/7 schedule. More recently, only five tenders work four 10-hour shifts between 6:30 AM and 5:00 PM. One tender works shorter hours and covers weekends, but one of them is always "on call" for off-hours openings. Averaging about thirty openings per bridge per month keep them hopping from one span to another. As tenders, they also see to other routine bridge maintenance chores, including work on the Astoria Bridge, but are always available to respond to watercraft needing to cross beneath the spans of the three movable bridges. With only five tenders to pull each shift, not all the bridges can be manned at one time. When a boat needs to pass, it puts in a call by shortwave radio or phone to the maintenance office. Since most passages require opening two bridges, one to allow a boat in or out of the bay from either Youngs River or Lewis and Clark River, and one to let it out of Youngs Bay or back in from the Columbia River, one of the bridge tenders typically drives from the office to each of the bridges needed to

YOUNGS BAY BRIDGE
Technical Data

Location: Astoria, Clatsop County; Oregon Coast Highway (US 101), Milepost 4.9

Year completed: 1964

Type: Vertical lift steel pony truss

Length: 4,129 feet

Deck to streambed: 75 feet

Description: Four 74-foot, twenty 80-foot prestressed reinforced-concrete deck girder spans, one 148-foot steel pony truss, one 153-foot vertical lift steel pony truss, two 55-foot, twenty 80-foot, two 74-foot, one 80-foot, and one 74-foot prestressed reinforced-concrete deck girder spans

Bridge engineer: Ivan D. Merchant

Cost: $4,250,000

Ownership: State of Oregon

Aerial view of the open vertical lift span.

be opened. There's a certain routine to it, but after watching for a while, every opening seems a little different, especially when the tide shifts or there's stormy weather.[2]

For bridge lovers, a midway stop on Youngs Bay Bridge provides a unique vantage point. From this spot, three other significant bridges can be seen—the towering Columbia River Bridge to the northeast and the two wonderful McCullough antiques profiled in the next chapter, Old Youngs Bay Bridge and Lewis and Clark River Bridge, that can be seen to the east and southeast respectively across Youngs Bay.

Youngs Bay was named for Sir George Young of the British Royal Navy by Lieutenant William Robert Broughton of George Vancouver's expedition, who discovered and explored Youngs Bay in October 1792. Young had an illustrious career with the navy, was knighted in 1781, and became an admiral in 1799.[3]

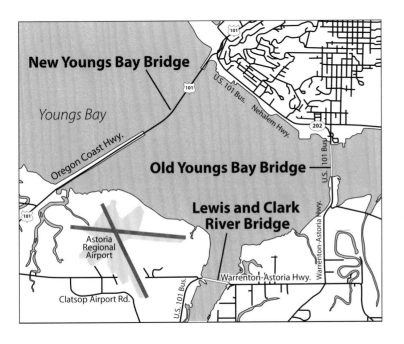

Two Early Conde B. McCullough Treasures

Old Youngs Bay Bridge and its nearby companion, the Lewis and Clark River Bridge, two classic bascule bridges designed in the 1920s by Conde B. McCullough, are well worth the slight detour off US 101 to visit them. Taken from the French word for "seesaw," bascules are counterbalanced drawbridges for easy raising or lowering. These classy, classic bridges are two of the finest old bascules to be found anywhere. Old Youngs Bay displays a double-leaf (two-section) bridge, while the Lewis and Clark River Bridge employs a single-leaf (one-section) bridge.

These must-see bridges are located on Warrenton Highway (OR 105/US 101B) that, until the new Youngs Bay Bridge was constructed in 1964, provided the main route south from Astoria. Today, sitting on a secondary highway, in a relatively unpopulated area, they remain protected from the heavy traffic of US 101, which has helped to extend their life. Hopefully they will be further protected by designation as historic landmarks.

Old Youngs Bay Bridge, Conde B. McCullough's oldest existing coastal bridge, as it appears looking west.

16

Old Youngs Bay Bridge
CLASSIC DOUBLE-LEAF BASCULE

Old Youngs Bay Bridge, a double-leaf bascule, remains Conde B. McCullough's oldest existing coastal bridge and, so far as we know, one of his first movable-span bridges. Nearly a century old at this writing and still in excellent working condition, the bridge raises and lowers daily, primarily for commercial fishing boats working off the mouth of the Columbia River. Recent work has improved its overall condition.

In a 1922 letter to U.S. National Bank President J.C. Ainsworth, one of Portland's early power brokers, regarding some bridge work he was applying for in Multnomah County, McCullough wrote that his experience includes "the design and construction of several rather good-sized movable bridges, including a 'double-leaf electrically operated bascule bridge at Youngs Bay.'"

He also mentioned that "Thomas H. MacDonald, chief of the federal Bureau of Public Roads [and an early mentor of McCullough's], visited the Youngs Bay structure last year and pronounced it to be one of the finest examples of movable highway bridges in the United States. Mr. MacDonald went so far as to state that he considered this structure to be 'a distinct advance in the art of highway bridge building.'"[1] Clearly, both MacDonald and McCullough shared a high opinion of the bridge and its designer.

Operator's house on Old Youngs Bay Bridge.

OLD YOUNGS BAY BRIDGE
Technical Data

Location: Astoria vicinity, Clatsop County;
Warrenton Highway
(OR 105), Milepost 6.8

Year completed: 1921

Type: Steel double-leaf bascule

Length: Total span 1,766 feet, central span
150 feet

Deck to streambed: 55 feet

Description: Two 23-foot and twenty-four
29-foot pile trestles, one 150-foot steel bascule
double-leaf draw span (250-ton), twenty-three
29-foot and nine 23-foot pile trestles

Cost: $170,000

Designer: Conde B. McCullough

Ownership: State of Oregon

Bridge as it appeared during construction.

Detail view of one of the bridge pylons which are featured at both ends of the bridge.

The bridge features a 150-foot central draw span with a steel double leaf bascule—two 75-foot, cantilevered sections. Originally operated by 40-horsepower electric motors and counterweights, new state of the art electronic equipment has replaced the dated original gear. Also, in 2010 the concrete deck was replaced with a steel grate.

Tall obelisk entrance pylons that became McCullough trademarks stand in pairs at each end of the bridge. These early pylons are unusual in that while made of concrete, they sport wood panels and are topped with lanterns to illuminate the bridge entrances. When the lanterns fell into disrepair the bridge maintenance crew built exact replicas. Entrance pylons continued to be used by McCullough (they are featured on all his major coastal bridges), but over time they became mostly decorative, made only of concrete, and usually without lanterns.

View of the The Lewis and Clark River Bridge as it appears looking northwest.

Lewis and Clark River Bridge

CLASSIC SINGLE-LEAF BASCULE

The Lewis and Clark River Bridge, a single-leaf bascule, endures as another of Conde B. McCullough's earliest movable coastal bridges. Completed in 1924, it remains the only pre-World War II single-leaf bascule span on the Oregon highway system.[1]

The bridge's total length is 828 feet. It features a 150-ton steel single-leaf bascule central draw span 112 feet long, flanked by 716 feet of timber-frame approach trestles. When opened, the bridge allows a horizontal waterway clearance of 105 feet. Its original electrical system has been completely renovated with state-of-the-art electronic gear.

Detail view of the bridge's truss work.

LEWIS AND CLARK RIVER BRIDGE

Technical Data

Location: Astoria Vicinity, Clatsop County; Warrenton Highway (OR 105), Milepost 4.7

Year completed: 1924

Type: Steel single-leaf bascule

Length: Total span 828 feet, central Span 112 feet

Deck to streambed: 23 feet

Description: Twenty-eight, 19-foot and one 14-foot treated timber-frame trestles, one 112-foot steel single-leaf bascule draw span (150-ton), one 18-foot and eight 19-foot treated timber-frame trestles

Designer: Conde B. McCullough

Contractor: Pacific Bridge Company, Portland, Oregon

Neawanna Creek Bridge as it appears looking southeast.

Neawanna Creek Bridge
A HARDY CROSS ORIGINAL

Neawanna Creek Bridge distinguishes itself as an intact example of a 1930s continuous concrete multi-span highway bridge that utilizes Hardy Cross's moment distribution method of analysis, and for its association with Conde B. McCullough, Oregon's premier bridge engineer.[1]

NEAWANNA CREEK BRIDGE
Technical Data

Location: Seaside vicinity, Clatsop County; Oregon Coast Highway (US 101), Milepost: 19.7

Year completed: 1930

Type: Reinforced-concrete deck girder

Length: 208 feet

Deck to streambed: 18 feet

Description: Four 52-foot reinforced-concrete deck girder spans with 5-foot sidewalks

Designer: Conde B. McCullough

Ownership: State of Oregon

The configuration of the continuous concrete T-beam construction used in the design of this 1930 bridge represents a significant change in structural engineering theory and reinforced-concrete technology by applying the moment distribution method of distributing loads as they move across girder structures.

One of the most important figures in American structural engineering in the early twentieth century, Cross developed new and practical methods of structural analysis that greatly simplified the way stresses could be calculated for continuous beams and frames. "Essentially, what Cross's methods did was simplify the monumental mathematical task of calculating innumerable equations to solve complex problems in the fields of structural and civil engineering, long before the computer age."[2] Today, his methods are no longer commonly used since computers have changed the way engineers calculate structural engineering problems.

Neawanna represents the third significant early bridge designed by Conde B. McCullough in the Astoria-Seaside area. Each serves to demonstrate McCullough's advanced engineering skills and utilization of innovative bridge technology.

The Necanicum River Bridge's reinforced-concrete deck arch employs three spandrel barrel-type sections.

Necanicum River (Seaside) Bridge

MAIL ORDER BRIDGE

Known as the "Broadway Bridge" in Seaside, this Necanicum River span sits on Broadway Street a few blocks west of US 101. One of the earliest surviving bridges along the Oregon coast, it is truly unique among Oregon's bridges.

The bridge showcases the product of Daniel B. Luten, an engineer and bridge designer from Indianapolis, Indiana, who designed and nationally marketed reinforced-concrete bridges during the early decades of the twentieth century. The only known Luten span in Oregon, this reinforced-concrete deck arch employs three 41-foot filled spandrel barrel-type sections, including half-arch approaches. Urn-shaped balusters support the railings, with lampposts at the approaches.[1]

According to *The Oregonian*, Luten filed suit against bridge contractors J.H. Tillman and L.A. Webster for an alleged $3,080 due him as royalty on the design of the bridge, maintaining that 10 percent of the contract price was to be paid to the designers (these suits apparently were common). It's unknown whether or not he ever collected.[2]

When the Necanicum River Bridge opened in 1924, a bronze bas-relief plaque entitled "Old Oregon Trail" by Oregon sculptor Avard Fairbanks was affixed to a centerpiece on the south railing and remains there today.[3] A companion plaque planned for the north railing was never added because of a lack of city funds to pay for it. Sixty-nine years later, in 1993, using federal urban renewal funds, the Seaside Improvement Commission approved $4,000 to commission the planned but never executed second plaque, a depiction of the Lewis and Clark salt works originally located

Plaque depicting the old Oregon Trail.

NECANICUM RIVER BRIDGE
Technical Data

Location: Broadway Street, Seaside, Clatsop County

Year completed: 1924

Type: Reinforced-concrete deck arch; three 41-foot filled spandrel, barrel-type sections, including half-arch approaches

Length: 123 feet

Designer: Daniel B. Luten

Ownership: City of Seaside

Plaque depicting Lewis and Clark salt works.

down river from the bridge site. The plaque, designed by I.A. Cox (also known as Leanne Waterhouse), finally "completed" the bridge.[4]

Seaside, Oregon's first coastal resort, got its name from an early hostelry, the Sea Side House, built by railroad tycoon Ben Holladay in 1873.[5]

The Necanicum River Bridge lies a few blocks west of US 101 and allows Broadway Street to continue to its oceanside destination.

The Necarney Creek Bridge looking north.

Necarney Creek (Samuel G. Reed) Bridge

TOWER OF POWER

Set within beautiful Oswald West State Park on the northern slopes of Neahkahnie Mountain, Necarney Creek Bridge demonstrates an unusual example of a relatively uncommon bridge type, the steel tower bridge. Constructed in 1937, it became the first of only two tower bridges built along the coast (Thomas Creek is the other). Its towers rise 85 feet above the creek bed and support the steel deck girders that carry the 602-foot roadway across the steep ravine.

Although constructed when traffic moved more slowly, its unusual, slightly banked and curved roadway was so skillfully engineered by then state bridge engineer Glenn S. Paxson that even with the higher speeds common today it's still easy to negotiate. In fact, if it weren't for the "period" concrete Gothic arch balustrade railings that belie its true age, Necarney Creek could easily pass for a bridge newer by decades. A close look at the railings today reveals considerable deterioration. They are now painted periodically in order to preserve them.

Dedicated to Samuel G. Reed on August 29, 1938, the bridge became a tribute to his thirty-year campaign to construct a road over Neahkahnie Mountain. A long-time resident of the area, Reed reputedly owned more than 1,000 acres on the mountain by 1911. In 1916 he built the Neahkahnie Tavern and soon after began promoting road construction.

Elected a Tillamook county commissioner in 1924, he succeeded in getting a gravel road built to within three miles of the existing Clatsop County road that ran south from Seaside. Reed later worked out a deal with the state whereby he would donate nearly one hundred acres and sell the state another two hundred in order to create Oswald West State Park. For this invaluable property the state agreed to pay $3,500 in taxes owing on the property and allowed Reed to continue grazing his sheep on Neahkahnie's mountain slopes.[1]

The park is named for Oregon's fourteenth governor, famously known for keeping Oregon's beaches in the public domain by making them a state highway. Oswald West State Park, one of the coast's finest scenic waysides, features tranquil walking trails and hike-in campsites with wheelbarrows for hauling gear, courtesy of the Oregon Parks and Recreation Department. A walk up the creek from the parking area reveals a beautiful waterfall. Downstream, Short Sands Beach has become one of Oregon's favorite surfing spots. A small suspension footbridge crosses the creek on the way to the beach, the only known example of this bridge type along the coast.

NECARNEY CREEK BRIDGE
Technical Data

Location: Arch Cape vicinity; Oregon Coast Highway (US 101), Milepost 39.5

Year completed: 1937

Type: Steel deck girder on steel towers

Length: 602 feet

Deck to streambed: 85 feet

Description: Series of six (50-foot suspended and 42-foot continuous) steel deck girders, and one 50-foot suspended steel deck girder span on steel towers (382-ton); the concrete deck is 26 feet wide with 3.5-foot sidewalks and Gothic arch balustrade railings

Engineer: Glenn S. Paxson

Ownership: State of Oregon

The WPA stonework on the Chasm Bridge gives the box girder construction the appearance of an arch.

8

Chasm (Neahkahnie Mountain) Bridge

HIDDEN TREASURE

According to legend there's buried treasure on Neahkahnie Mountain but, as far as we know, no one has found it. Yet anyone can discover the hidden highway treasure Chasm Bridge just by looking. Perched atop a ledge chiseled out of solid rock, this faux-arched bridge is an integral part of the highway that traverses the mountain's steep ocean face nine hundred feet above the surf. This spectacular "high-wire" highway construction project around Neahkahnie Mountain displays another prime example of the remarkable engineering feats performed by the federal Works Progress Administration (WPA) during the Great Depression of the 1930s. This bridge and roadway, completed in 1937, spanned the last major headland to be crossed by the Oregon Coast Highway.[1]

Using hand-cut stonework to help support the highway and provide roadside railings on the ocean side, this unique stretch of US 101 demonstrates the high quality of WPA work. Running for nearly three-quarters of a mile, only the stonework railings are visible as one travels through the cut. The stonework continues below the highway, facing the ocean-side walls of the bridge and several half viaducts below the roadway, including the simple concrete girders that support the bridge, which gives it the appearance of an arched stone structure.

To see this unusual bridge, one must park in the popular roadside turnout and walk south beyond the large solitary stone pinnacle that sits on the outer edge of the roadway at Milepost

WPA workers face the Chasm Bridge arch with stone masonry in 1937.

40. By leaning over the rock railing, one can just see the bridge's outer arch. The cliffs here are steep and dangerous, requiring great caution. The turnout provides a spectacular view of the village of Manzanita and the broad stretch of beach running south to Nehalem Bay.

On the southern side of the parking area created by the stone wall that encircles the overlook sits a simple stone monument affixed with a bronze plaque bearing the following inscription:

Historic plaque commemorating Oregon Governor Oswald West.

IF SIGHT OF SAND AND SKY AND SEA
HAS GIVEN RESPITE FROM YOUR DAILY CARES
THEN PAUSE TO THANK
OSWALD WEST
FORMER GOVERNOR OF OREGON (1911-1915)

BY HIS FORESIGHT
NEARLY 400 MILES OF THE OCEAN SHORE
WAS SET ASIDE FOR PUBLIC USE
FROM THE COLUMBIA RIVER ON THE NORTH
TO THE CALIFORNIA BORDER TO THE SOUTH

THIS MARKER IS ERECTED AND DEDICATED
BY THE GRATEFUL CITIZENS OF OREGON
TO COMMEMORATE
THIS OUTSTANDING ACHIEVEMENT

Over the years, Chasm Bridge and the adjacent roadway have suffered frequent rock slides. In May and November of 1994, slides closed Neahkahnie Mountain to travel for several months. A 15-ton boulder nearly the size of a Volkswagen bug became the most spectacular piece of debris that cascaded down onto the roadway. After extensive work to re-sculpt the highway cut along the steep, rock-faced mountainside and make some road repairs, the highway has been largely trouble free.[2]

Neahkahnie Mountain, known by the Tillamook Indians as the "home of the gods," became a landmark for early European mariners seeking the Northwest Passage and other discoveries. It remains today a spiritual place of legend, romance, intrigue, and treasure, in part because of these early European mariners whose mysterious leavings, such as bundles of beeswax and stones with undecipherable markings found throughout the area, have only added to Neahkahnie's allure.[3]

CHASM BRIDGE

Technical Data

Location: Manzanita vicinity, Tillamook County; Oregon Coast Highway (US 101), Milepost 40.7

Year completed: 1937

Type: Reinforced-concrete deck girder

Length: 102 feet

Deck to streambed: 57 feet

Description: One 13-foot reinforced-concrete slab span, one 59-foot reinforced-concrete deck girder span, three 10-foot reinforced-concrete slab spans, one 3.5-foot sidewalk

Designer: Glenn S. Paxson

Ownership: State of Oregon

To the casual observer, Chasm Bridge remains virtually hidden as from this on-deck view traveling south, the town of Manzanita in the far distance.

The S-curve construction of the new Nehalem Bridge is apparent in this view looking west.

9

Nehalem River Bridge

ALAS, FORM FOLLOWS FUNCTION

The Nehalem River Bridge, located just south of the charming little town that bears the river's name, represents one of several medium-sized, reinforced-concrete replacement bridges built along the coast over the last several decades. Constructed in 1983, this box girder span's thin profile and graceful S curve make it one of the more interesting and attractive of these newer bridges.

Built here, however, in part to provide sufficient clearance for occasional river traffic, it seems oversized for the lovely site it graces. The Oregon Department of Transportation deemed the old bridge's narrow width and lack of pedestrian walkways a safety hazard. If true, the benefit of the new bridge's roadway, apparently built for speed, seems puzzling. Traffic has to slow to get into Nehalem heading north, and has already slowed passing through town heading south. Couldn't walkways and/or bikeways have been added on the outside of the old bridge?

The new span replaced one of the coast's last steel-swing spans, a distinctive local landmark. Built in 1921, its steel truss style matched hundreds of Oregon bridges built during the 1920s and 1930s, most of which have now disappeared. Unlike many of the new and larger reinforced-concrete replacement bridges, the old steel bridges provided a more attractive

Bridge as seen from the north.

NEHALEM RIVER BRIDGE
Technical Data

Location: Nehalem vicinity, Tillamook County; Oregon Coast Highway (US 101), Milepost 45.6

Year completed: 1983

Type: Reinforced-concrete box girder

Length: 1,062 feet

Deck to streambed: 80 feet

Description: Two 180-foot and three 234-foot post tens box girder spans

Contractor: F.E. Ward Inc., Vancouver, WA

Ownership: State of Oregon

Historic view of original Nehalem Bridge looking northeast.

superstructure. They also fit comfortably into small communities like Nehalem and brought a simple charm that enhanced the setting. Without a doubt, the old bridge provided a much more attractive backdrop to Nehalem, especially when viewed from the decks of local restaurants that back up to the river.

As Conde B. McCullough's bridges remind us, the best bridges are both well engineered and designed to enhance the beauty of the sites they span. Since contemporary bridges will be our companions for many generations, we should be as concerned with their aesthetic qualities as we are about making them efficient and durable.

View of Nehalem Bridge looking northwest.

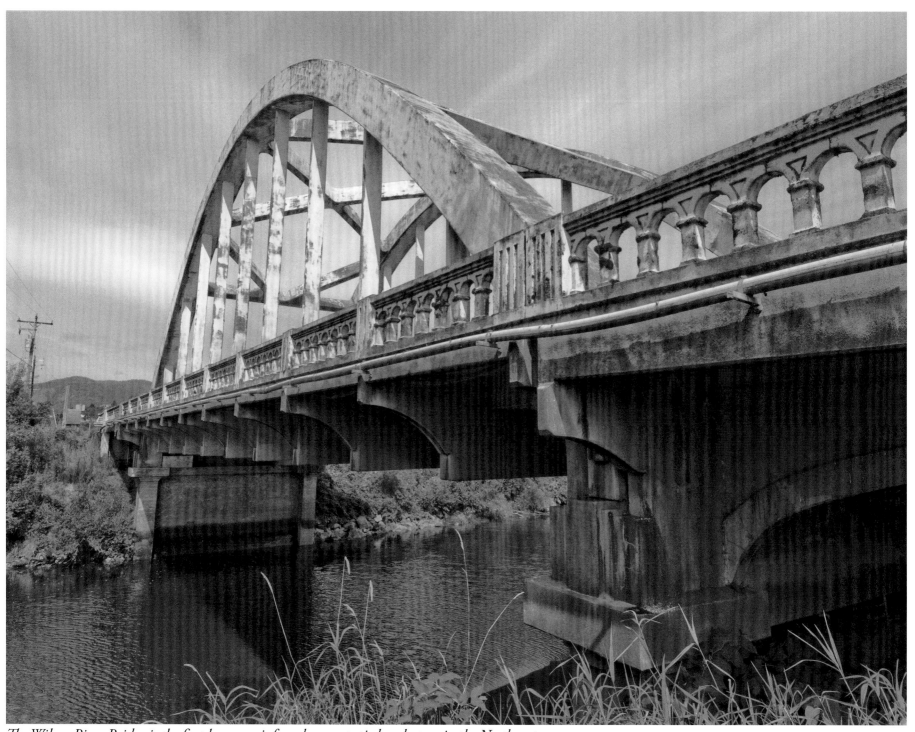

The Wilson River Bridge is the first known reinforced-concrete tied-arch span in the Northwest.

10

Wilson River Bridge

TIED-ARCH PIONEER

The Wilson River, named for an early settler who first brought cows into Tillamook County and founded the dairy industry made famous by Tillamook Cheese, also names the hallmark local bridge designed by Conde B. McCullough.[1] Located on the northern outskirts of the town of Tillamook, the Wilson River Bridge is often referred to as the "Historic Bridge" by Tillamook residents and adds a little sparkle to this placid inland segment of the Oregon Coast Highway.

Wilson River Bridge became the first known reinforced-concrete tied-arch span in the Northwest.[2] Because the horizontal thrust of the arch is constrained by the deck, much like the string holds the expansion of an archer's bow, the tied arch is often referred to as the "bow-string" or "rainbow" arch. This construction technique differed from the traditional fixed arch bridges that required massive abutments to withstand the arch's pressure. The tied arch was used here and in the Big Creek and Tenmile Creek bridges farther south because there was no natural solid rock formation upon which to abut a traditional arch bridge, such as at Depoe Bay.

McCullough apparently learned this technique during his tenure with the Marsh Construction Company of Des Moines, Iowa, prior to coming to Oregon in 1916. Founder James B. Marsh created and patented a reinforced-concrete "rainbow" arch bridge in 1912 that was replicated throughout Iowa and Kansas during the early twentieth century. These examples became some of the earliest tied-arch bridges in the country.[3]

McCullough's versions are slightly different in that he used the Considère hinge, rather than the steel plates and latticework used by Marsh. Designed by French engineer Armand Considère, the hinge uses a concentration of steel reinforcing bar to channel the loads of the center of the arch ribs, giving them more flexibility. Since the tied arch was still a relatively new concept when McCullough built his coastal bridges, his innovations helped further the development of reinforced-concrete arch bridge construction.

View of plaque on the Wilson River Bridge.

WILSON RIVER BRIDGE
Technical Data

Location: Tillamook vicinity, Tillamook County; Oregon Coast Highway (US 101), Milepost 64.7

Year completed: 1931

Type: Reinforced-concrete through tied arch

Length: 180 feet

Deck to streambed: 33 feet

Description: One 30-foot, reinforced-concrete deck girder span, one 120-foot, reinforced-concrete through tied arch, one 30-foot reinforced-concrete deck girder span, and 3.5-foot sidewalks

Designer: Conde B. McCullough

Contractor: Clackamas Construction Company

Ownership: State of Oregon

Original arch of bridge featured x bracing.

Original view of Wilson River Bridge facing north.

West Beaver Creek Bridge remains the oldest existing bridge on the Oregon Coast Highway.

West Beaver Creek Bridge

ORIGINAL COUNTY RELIC

Tucked into one of the more remote inland sections of US 101, this unpretentious little bridge may easily be overlooked as motorists wind their way along the luscious farmland of Tillamook County. But don't be fooled by lack of pretense, for West Beaver Creek is a very unique bridge. For starters, this rare little span constructed in 1914 remains the oldest existing bridge on the Oregon Coast Highway. It's also one of the last surviving original county bridges constructed before the development of the Oregon State Highway System still in use on a major state highway. As of this writing, this bridge has served us for nearly one hundred years.

The Oregon State Highway Commission and the Oregon State Highway Department were created in 1913, about the time Tillamook County began construction of the West Beaver Creek Bridge, charged with developing a comprehensive state highway system. Oregon's roads were then a hodgepodge of local and county roads and bridges such as West Beaver Creek, which remains one of the few still serving the Oregon Coast Highway.

Its early and undistinguished birth is reflected in its design. Other than the recessed railing panels and extended rail caps, the only decorative embellishments on this reinforced-concrete structure are the 1914 date of construction engraved in the east side bridge railing panel and the names of county judge Homer Mason and county commissioner H.M. Farmer on the west railing.

The main span of West Beaver Creek Bridge is a single 65-foot filled spandrel, rib type reinforced-concrete deck arch with no approach structures. The 1914 arch, still visible on the west side of the bridge, originally supported only a narrow 16- to 18-foot roadway. The bridge was widened in 1935 with two 22-foot reinforced-concrete deck girders along the east side of the arch.[1]

Undoubtedly, highway widening and straightening will eventually require abandoning or replacing these old bridges, but for now they still serve us well, both as current working bridges and as historic links to an earlier era of coastal highway travel.

WEST BEAVER CREEK BRIDGE

Technical Data

Location: Beaver vicinity, Tillamook County; Oregon Coast Highway (US 101), Milepost 77.5

Year completed: 1914; widened in 1935

Type: Reinforced-concrete arch

Length: 65 feet

Deck to streambed: 10 feet

Description: One 65-foot concrete spandrel arch; widened with two 22-foot reinforced-concrete deck girder spans

Owner: State of Oregon

Drift Creek Bridge on its new location across Bear Creek.

Drift Creek Bridge

COVERED BRIDGE MIRACLE

For lovers of covered bridges, one of Oregon's oldest can be found on Bear Creek Road, five miles east of US 101 off Oregon Highway 18. How did Drift Creek Bridge get to Bear Creek? Therein lays the miracle.

Drift Creek Bridge originally sat on Drift Creek County Road, then a main north-south route along the early coast highway south of Lincoln (Cutler) City, just a couple of miles off today's US 101. This highway section was bypassed when the original Oregon Coast Highway was completed in 1932. The original bridge, thought to have been constructed in 1914 at a cost of $1,800, utilized a timber through truss (Howe) span 66 feet in length. It sported flared board-and-batten siding, arched portals, ribbon daylighting, and wooden plank flooring.[1]

A similar bridge over Schooner Creek in nearby Taft needed to be replaced in 1945 because it couldn't survive the heavy traffic along the coast highway. Shielded from the traffic of US 101, Drift Creek Bridge survived for decades, but didn't get the attention needed to keep it sound. By the mid-1960s, the bridge was closed to vehicular traffic and bypassed by a concrete span constructed immediately down river that is still in use. It reopened in 1965 following a restoration, but only for pedestrian traffic.

After years of benign neglect, the bridge continued to deteriorate. In 1988, the county closed the bridge even to pedestrian traffic. Steel beams were installed inside the bridge just to keep it from falling into the river. After repeated debate, in 1997 the Lincoln County Commission voted to demolish the bridge.[2]

Laura and Kerry Sweitz, who live a few miles north of the original Drift Creek Bridge site on Bear Creek Road off Oregon Highway 18, learned of the commissioners' decision on September 14, 1997. They had just constructed a concrete bridge across Bear Creek to reach their home site, but as Laura remembers it, when they heard the news about Drift Creek Bridge being demolished, "Our minds raced and the miracles began." The first thing they did was to measure their existing bridge, which turned out to be 66 feet 10 inches long and 16 feet wide, nearly the exact dimensions of Drift Creek Bridge.

Knowing that the bridge would fit on their property, the Sweitzes requested and received a special hearing from the commissioners. They promised that for no cost they would "…re-erect the house portion of the old bridge…and give the public easement for heritage purposes for all time." Without stopping the demolition, the commissioners granted their request and "miraculously" gave the bridge remains to the Sweitzes.

And so the dismantled bridge—in hundreds of pieces—came to reside with the Sweitzes, who struggled to find a way to reconstruct it on their property. Building, or rebuilding a bridge, even on your own property, takes plans, engineering, and money—lots of it. The Sweitzes did what they could with their limited resources, milling rafters and hand-splitting cedar shakes for the roof. Other help came from fundraisers and

45

DRIFT CREEK BRIDGE
Technical Data

Location: Current site: The bridge is located off Oregon 18, 4.96 miles east of US 101 on Bear Creek Road. (Original site: Cutler City vicinity, Lincoln County, Drift Creek County Road, east of US 101.)

Year completed: Uncertain: 1914 or 1933

Type: Timber through truss (Howe) covered bridge

Length: 66 feet

Description: 66-foot housed Howe truss, with flared board-and-batten siding, arched portals, ribbon daylighting, and wooden plank flooring

Ownership: Laura and Kerry Sweitz

Bridge as seen on original location.

supporters. The Simpson Timber Company donated the three huge beams needed to support the bridge, and Hull-Oaks Lumber Company milled them to their proper size.

After four years of what can only be described as an extraordinary labor of love, on July 14, 2001, the Sweitzes delivered a fully reconstructed bridge. More than half of the reconstructed bridge uses original bridge material, including wooden slats from the bridge's interior with graffiti memorializing marriage proposals, love, and the first fish caught. The cornerstone was donated by Taft Masonic Lodge No. 200.[3]

The Sweitzes donated the bridge and the land upon which it rests to Lincoln County and made the bridge available to visitors 365 days a year. It now stands as a memorial to its twentieth-century pioneer builders and, thankfully, to its twenty-first century saviors.

New information regarding the age of the Drift Creek Bridge surfaced during the dismantling of the old bridge. Algrid Zaplys, contractor in charge of the project, and Steve Wyatt, Lincoln County Historical Society curator, discovered anomalies in the construction materials.

Though research continues, the new evidence suggests that the existing bridge replaced an earlier damaged one and was likely constructed in 1933 by James V. Curry.[4] Either way, we're lucky to have this historic structure restored.

Interior of bridge before restoration.

The Siletz River Bridge as seen from the west.

A FACE ONLY A MOTHER COULD LOVE

This behemoth of a bridge, birthed in controversy, drew fire from all sides. Local homeowners in the Siletz Key development west of the highway protested because the proposed bridge was too high, while tugboat operators argued that the bridge was too low—they wanted one high enough to allow commercial boats to navigate beneath it.[1] Some voiced concern because it would replace the historic Kernville Bridge designed by Conde B. McCullough. Still others maintained that there might be adverse ecological effects on Siletz Bay.[2]

The Siletz River Bridge reflects a popular trend in the 1960s and 1970s, when reinforced concrete became the preferred method of bridge construction. Building on the innovations of McCullough's generation, new technologies in concrete, reinforcing steel, and freeway construction methods enabled the production of relatively inexpensive and flexible highway structures. These techniques dominated bridge construction during this era, and not always in a positive way. Where designers might have opted for a more delicate touch, such as with the Chetco River Bridge, massive structures like the Siletz were often the final product.

Emulating the glamour of a freeway overpass, this bridge demonstrates how a beautiful site can be overwhelmed by a monolithic structure devoid of any sense of place, scale, or design. In contrast to the bridge it replaced, it offers little to its environment except faster traffic. It is one of only a handful of four-lane coastal bridges, hardly a necessity here, since a two-lane highway flanks it at both ends. Fortunately for the residents of the Siletz Key development, the underpinnings of the bridge are a bit more graceful than its unsightly highway face.

The Chetco River Bridge in Brookings (1972) and the more recent Alsea Bay Bridge (1991) demonstrate a sharp contrast with the Siletz. These two award-winning reinforced-concrete bridges exemplify the quality

SILETZ RIVER BRIDGE

Technical Data

Location: Lincoln City vicinity, Lincoln County; Oregon Coast Highway (US 101), Milepost 120.1

Year completed: 1973

Type: Reinforced-concrete box girder

Length: 920 feet

Deck to streambed: 55 feet

Description: One 130-foot, four 165-foot and one 130-foot reinforced-concrete box girder spans with a 30-degree skew and 5-foot sidewalks

Ownership: State of Oregon

that can be achieved for little additional cost. As older coastal structures are replaced, it remains to be seen whether the new bridges will look like the Chetco and Alsea Bay or the Siletz. But, recent replacement bridges such as Cooks Chasm and Brush Creek demonstrate that a new design-conscious bridge design team now reigns at the Oregon Department of Transportation.

Interestingly, when the old Kernville Bridge was replaced, the new bridge became the Siletz River Bridge. With that name change, the Kernville community connection died as well. According to *Oregon Geographic Names,* Daniel and John Kern founded the Kern Brothers Packing Company in 1896, a salmon cannery located on the north bank of the river a mile or two inland

from the mouth of the Siletz River.[3] By providing local fisherman with boats and nets and offering to buy all the fish they could catch, Daniel Kern made a lot of local farmers happy by giving them a more enjoyable and profitable way to make a living. The enterprise became North Lincoln County's first major industry and the community that grew up around it, on both sides of the river,

The four-lane bridge deck is supported by massive concrete underpinnings.

The original Kernville bridge with debris from flood water.

became a town. When a new post office opened John Kern became its first postmaster.

According to Anne Hall, director of the North Lincoln County Historical Society, "The new bridge took commerce and industry away from Kernville. As a result, most of Old Kernville has disappeared over the years, replaced by homes and fishing cabins."[4] Even a well-known restaurant just east of the bridge, bearing the Kernville name on its roof, finally closed in 2009.

Another local landmark, often called the "movie house," sits on the south bank of the river about a mile east of the bridge. Best viewed from Kernville Road on the north side of the river, the original house served as a prop for the movie adaptation of Oregonian Ken Kesey's novel, *Sometimes a Great Notion*. After several upgrades, the house has finally been converted into a real home.[5]

The Depoe Bay Bridge bears the distinction of being Conde B. McCullough's first reinforced-concrete arch coastal bridge design.

Depoe Bay Bridge

OSCAR WINNER

Depoe Bay's harbor, proclaimed locally as the "world's smallest harbor," and the Depoe Bay Bridge that spans the harbor's narrow inlet, receive co-billing as the major attractions of this busy little tourist town. Together they form a three-dimensional intersection, with water traffic crossing beneath the land traffic above. On any given day a lot of activity takes place on both levels.

When Conde B. McCullough constructed his first reinforced-concrete arch bridge along the coast at Depoe Bay in 1927, the town didn't exist. But the new bridge soon attracted both commercial and residential investors who saw opportunity and purchased land around the bridge with the intention of turning the area into a town site. Before long, Depoe Bay was on its way to becoming a popular coastal tourist attraction.[1]

The original bridge featured a 150-foot single span reinforced-concrete deck arch, which crosses the narrow inlet to the bay. The 18-foot wide roadway did not include sidewalks. In 1940 an additional arch rib widened the bridge to the west, duplicating the arch design of the original structure. The widening wasn't intended to accommodate more automobile traffic; rather, it provided space for the growing crowds of pedestrian traffic that congregated along the Gothic bridge railings to watch the boats charge the bay's treacherous rocky inlet.[2]

The unique dual bridge arches are easily viewed from a sidewalk underpass accessed by a stairway at the north end of the bridge or, for a price, from one of the charter fishing or sightseeing boats that pass beneath it daily. From below it's easy to see how the bridge's arches are supported by skewback sections connected to solid rock. Also note the

Adding additional lanes on the Depoe Bay Bridge in 1940.

DEPOE BAY BRIDGE
Technical Data

Location: Depoe Bay, Lincoln County; Oregon Coast Highway (US 101), Milepost 127.6

Year completed: 1927

Type: Reinforced-concrete deck arch

Length: 312 feet

Deck to streambed: 100 feet

Description: One 29-foot reinforced deck girder approach span, one 150-foot reinforced-concrete deck arch main span, and three 40-foot and one 13-foot reinforced deck girder approach spans

Designer: Conde B. McCullough

Contractor: Kuckenberg-Wittman Company, Portland, Oregon

Cost: $55,557

Ownership: State of Oregon

1940 BRIDGE WIDENING PROJECT

Contractor: Odom Construction Co.,

Cost: $60,367

Renovation contract: Cathodic protection system installed in 1995

Trusswork on underside of the bridge.

View of the Depoe Bay Bridge facing west during construction of additional lanes, 1940.

wood grain impressions left in the concrete by the construction forms. The precast railings consist of small arched openings with a band of dentils under the railing. The stairway also provides access to a public park building in Depoe Bay State Park.[3]

The town's name continues to be a bit of a mystery. The most reliable accounts suggest that the town was named for Siletz Indian William DePoe and his wife Matilda, who established title to about two hundred acres around where the town now sits. After their death, heirs sold the property to developers who created the town.[4]

Movie buffs may recognize the bridge and harbor from the 1975 Oscar-winning movie, *One Flew Over the Cuckoo's Nest,* adapted from Ken Kesey's novel.

Rocky Creek Bridge lies three miles south of Depoe Bay on a little-known US 101 bypass called Otter Crest Loop.

Rocky Creek (Ben F. Jones) Bridge

BYPASS SURGERY PATIENT

New visitors to the coast often miss Rocky Creek Bridge, a favorite of coastal bridge enthusiasts, because it sits on Otter Crest Loop, once part of the Oregon Coast Highway but now a little-known US 101 bypass three miles south of Depoe Bay. One of Conde B. McCullough's earliest and most appealing coastal bridges, this graceful reinforced-concrete arch spans the rocky gorge that names it and creates a striking counterpoint to the jagged lava formations below.

Completed in 1927, the bridge now seems too narrow for conventional two-way traffic, but its 20-foot width (two feet wider than the original Depoe Bay Bridge) is consistent with the highway construction standards of its era. The bridge's 360-foot length features a 160-foot central rib deck arch perfectly balanced between five 20-foot reinforced-concrete deck girder spans on either end.

By the 1980s, preservationists and bridge maintenance crews became concerned because its serious state of deterioration made its future questionable.[1] Load limits were imposed when the bridge's reinforcing bar became exposed, the result of cracking and spalling concrete, similar to the problems that afflicted the old Alsea Bay Bridge.

The bridge, now completely rehabilitated at a cost of $4.5 million, includes an active cathodic protection system to fight corrosion and preserve the bridge for many decades to come. The only downside is that the zinc coating of the cathodic protection system, as at Cape Creek Bridge and others so treated, altered the bridge's original tan tones to slightly gray, a small price to pay for its salvation.[2]

Ben F. Jones, an early lawyer, legislator, and developer in the area, earned the title "Father of the Oregon Coast Highway" for his persistent efforts to build a highway along the coast. On September 17, 1927, two years after Jones's death, the bridge was dedicated in his name. In the 1970s, local boosters erected a historical marker to Jones with the following inscription:

> Where old US 101 crosses Rocky Creek, Ben Jones, pioneer lawyer, legislator and promoter, in 1907 purchased the Dope Spencer Indian Allotment where he developed the community of Otter Rock. Through the years he never ceased working to get a highway built along the coast, and in 1927 he was honored [posthumously] at a public ceremony at which this bridge was dedicated to him as the "Father of the Roosevelt Coast Highway."

After the restoration, a shorter new tribute was installed.

Otter Crest Loop, one of the few remaining remnants of the original Oregon Coast Highway completed in 1932, runs from Rocky Creek Bridge at the north end over Cape Foulweather to Otter Rock at the south end where it rejoins US 101. Driving this stretch of road offers a drive back through time. Heading south on the loop from the junction with US 101, the motorist slows to cross the narrow Rocky Creek Bridge, passes by the

ROCKY CREEK BRIDGE
Technical Data

Location: Otter Crest Loop, Miroco vicinity, Lincoln County; US 101 bypass, Milepost 130

Year completed: 1927

Type: Reinforced-concrete arch

Length: 360 feet

Description: Five 20-foot reinforced-concrete deck girders, one 160-foot reinforced-concrete deck arch, five 20-foot reinforced-concrete deck girder spans

Designer: Conde B. McCullough

Contractor: H.E. Doering, Portland

Ownership: State of Oregon

Renovation contract: Cathodic protection system installed in 2001

Bridge during construction.

small community of Miroco, then heads up the northern slope of Cape Foulweather through a sylvan glen replete with tight curves and steep, unguarded precipices looming just beyond the asphalt roadway. Although only a few miles in length, Otter Crest Loop allows motorists a chance to capture for a moment the experience of traveling the Oregon Coast Highway in its early years.

Over the last few decades, this old section of highway repeatedly suffered hits by major landslides that completely washed out the roadway. After one slide, a motorist and his son survived a harrowing plunge onto the slide area. Miraculously they escaped falling into the ocean and were rescued unharmed. Since then the road has been rebuilt for southbound motor traffic only.

The Rocky Creek Bridge features a central rib deck arch balanced between five reinforced-concrete deck girder spans on either end.

The Spencer Creek Bridge looking east.

Spencer Creek (Beverly Beach) Bridge

16

BEVERLY BEACH BEAUTY

The Spencer Creek Bridge just north of Newport, a 100-year structure completed in 2008 and one of the most recent significant coastal bridge to be constructed as of this writing, sits at the northern end of Beverly Beach. It is an integral part of Beverly Beach State Park, one of the most popular parks along the coast, and provides access to Beverly Beach through a bridge underpass.

Before the new bridge was built, there were increasing complaints about concrete chunks falling onto the pedestrian path under the bridge, caused by the severe deterioration of the old bridge. For safety concerns, the Oregon Department of Transportation (ODOT) removed portions of concrete from the underside of the bridge and installed safety netting to protect pedestrians.

The third deck-arch bridge to be constructed in the last ten years by the recently reinvigorated Bridge Section of ODOT, this dramatic open-spandrel bridge is less ornate than the more southern recent bridges, Cooks Chasm and Brush Creek. Three massive reinforced-concrete rib arches, each 140 feet long, bring a brawny beauty to the bridge. At the top of the deck, distinctive bas relief concrete railings reflect an arch design in a brown tone that contrasts with the original gray of the bridge arches. The only detractions are the artificial stone concrete panels that make up the retaining wall along the highway cut and the under-highway bulwarks. These appear to be catalogue bought and diminish the look of what is otherwise a very stunning bridge.

Replacement of the original Spencer Creek Bridge became necessary when in 1999 maintenance crews discovered that the 1947 reinforced-concrete bridge had severely deteriorated because of corrosion of the reinforcing steel in the bridge, caused by saltwater seeping into the concrete, a common problem along the coast. The bridge was deteriorating so quickly that even though weight limitations were imposed, a new temporary bridge had to be constructed and the old bridge removed from service.

Landslides have also plagued the Spencer Creek-Beverly Beach area for many years and are well documented in the environmental study prepared by ODOT in its planning to replace the old Spencer Creek Bridge. Creating a trouble-free structure along this eroding shoreline of landslide hazard that provides critical access to Beverly Beach State Park, the Beverly Beach shoreline, and the ocean-side community of Beverly Beach, became a major design challenge. (For readers interested in the colossal amount of preparation the department must do to construct a bridge along the coast, a visit to the Spencer Creek Bridge's environmental study on ODOT's website will be instructive.[1])

According to *Oregon Geographic Names*, Spencer Creek was named for Doke Spencer, a Native American who lived near its mouth. The beach's name apparently derived from the favorite doll of Florence Christy, daughter of Curtis and Florence Christy, who in the 1930s owned the property now known as Beverly Beach.[2]

SPENCER CREEK BRIDGE
Technical Data

Location: Newport vicinity, Lincoln County; Oregon Coast Highway (US 101), Milepost 133.86

Year completed: 2008

Type: Reinforced-concrete open-spandrel deck arch

Length: 210 feet

Deck to streambed: 45 feet

Description: Open-spandrel deck arch, three 140.1-foot open rib arches

Contractor: Slayden Construction

Ownership: State of Oregon

Detail view of the open-spandrel arches.

The Spencer Creek Bridge, viewed from the west, uses open-spandrel construction with three massive reinforced-concrete rib arches.

Perspective view of the Yaquina Bay Bridge looking south.

17

Yaquina Bay (Newport) Bridge

CENTERPIECE SPAN

The Yaquina Bay Bridge, one of Oregon's most famous landmarks, reigns as the centerpiece of the coast highway's unique bridge collection. Its towering steel arch creates a spectacular gateway for both motorists driving into Newport and mariners sailing into its scenic harbor. One of Conde B. McCullough's most iconic designs, the Yaquina became the last and northernmost of the five bridges built as part of the Oregon Coast Bridges Project financed by the federal Public Works Administration (PWA) during the Great Depression of the 1930s.

McCullough characterized the bridge site as "one of the most beautiful and spectacular settings imaginable. The north shore of the bay rises as a cliff, almost sheer, to a height of approximately 100 feet above the level of the bay, while on the south the partially wooded sand dunes extend down the coast as far as the eye can reach."[1] Of McCullough's major coastal bridges, often described as "jewel-like clasps in perfect settings, linking units of a beautiful highway," the Yaquina clearly shines as the crown jewel.[2]

Explaining his steel arch choice, McCullough wrote that he needed "to provide a 600-foot channel span for navigation which rendered the cost of concrete prohibitive. Our preliminary studies involved the consideration of several different cantilever arrangements and also a consideration of simple span types. The latticed half-through arch was selected largely for aesthetic reasons although no marked economy was shown in any of the other types considered."[3]

Heading south from the 100-foot cliff at the north end, the bridge roadway rises at a 4-percent grade, cresting midway through the central arch 140 feet above the water, while high above the roadway at this same point the top chords of the arch soar to 250 feet. From these central steel arches to the sandy beach at the southern end of the bay rise a series of five reinforced-concrete deck arches and seven reinforced-concrete deck girder spans, features McCullough often repeats in his larger coastal bridges.[4]

The Yaquina's opening completed Oregon's dream of an uninterrupted automobile route between the Columbia River and the California border, but it also ended forever the colorful but ultimately inefficient ferry service that served the Oregon Coast Highway for so many years. Only the ferry service across the Columbia River to Washington would continue until the opening of the Columbia River Bridge in 1966.[5]

The new bridge bypasses and crosses above Old Newport, which fronts the bay at its west end. To accommodate pedestrians, the bridge terminates with an Art Deco esplanade on the lofty north shore with graceful staircases that connect the bridge to Old Newport.

During its two-year construction phase, the Yaquina Bay Bridge employed about 220 laborers weekly, a significant boost to the central coast economy. Newport resident Paul Towsley, one of the men lucky

YAQUINA BAY BRIDGE
Technical Data

Location: Newport, Lincoln County; Oregon Coast Highway (US 101), Milepost 141.6

Year completed: 1936

Type: Steel half-through arch (top of arch 245 feet above bay)

Length: 3,323 feet

Deck to bay: 140 feet

Description: From the north end there are five reinforced-concrete deck girder spans of 51, 50, 57, 70, and 56 feet; one 350-foot steel deck arch; one 600-foot steel deck arch; one 350-foot steel deck arch; five reinforced-concrete deck arches 265, 232, 204,180, and 160 feet; and six reinforced-concrete deck girder spans 56, 70, 56.5, 70, 56.5, and 51 feet in length. There are two 3.5-foot sidewalks.

Designer: Conde B. McCullough

Bridge engineer: Conde B. McCullough

Arch designer: Ivan D. Merchant

Resident engineer: F.A. Furrow

Contractor: Bilpin Construction Company and General Construction Company, Otto Herman, Superintendent

Cost: $1,357,567

Ownership: State of Oregon

Renovation contract: Cathodic protection system installed in 1992

A man walks a girder during bridge construction.

enough to be employed on the bridge, described the work:

> Labor was slow…I went to work on the bridge in 1933, wheeling cement until 1936. They had walkways built out to where they was pouring cement; big ramps. They had a cement plant set up there at the end of the bridge that didn't shut down. It ran 24 hours a day. It stormed but they poured cement anyway. Sometimes it was so foggy that from the cement mixer you couldn't see out to where you were going to pour…I started to work for $.45 an hour, but there was a penny a day taken out for insurance compensation. Then they came along with this Townsend Plan and I signed up for social security. All of us had to get a social security number. That was in 1936. Then they started withholding a little bit more. [6]

Beyond the jobs provided during the Great Depression by the Oregon Coast Bridges Project, the year after the five bridges were completed, tourism along the coast jumped 72 percent in one year.[7]

The Yaquina Bay Bridge has benefited from two major restorations to extend its life. In 1980 it underwent a much-needed $10 million facelift that resulted in the first significant repair of the bridge in its then forty-year life. According to an article in the *Pacific Builder and Engineer*, "…the bridge is being bolstered by replacement of 1,300 feet of its deck, a contract that is

The main arch span as seen before construction links north to south in March of 1936.

Various ferries served Yaquina Bay from the 1880s to 1936 when the bridge was completed.

Stairway leading up to the bridge deck on the northwest side of the Yaquina Bridge displays the great attention to detail for which McCullough is noted.

Historic plaque lists creation date and contractors.

costing more than twice that of the original construction of the entire bridge" ($2.9 million compared to $1.3 million).[8]

The original concrete deck, sidewalk, and center span railings were replaced, allowing it to handle heavier modern traffic more safely. (The main span's deck is now a steel grate.) The concrete arches flanking the main span had cracked due to expansion of the corroding steel reinforcing bar and needed to be scaled away, and the exposed steel sandblasted, treated with epoxy, and resurfaced with concrete.

The decision to replace the ornate concrete railings caused considerable consternation among preservationists and bridge purists. Although the steel replacement railings convey the Gothic-arch theme of the originals, they likely would not have been approved had the bridge been on the National Register of Historic Places at that time.

The second project, begun in 1992, featured a three-year state-of-the-art cathodic protection project to protect the bridge from further deterioration. Adjusted for inflation, the $12 million price tag on this project was nearly nine

68

times the original bridge cost. Undoubtedly an expensive outlay, it seems a bargain compared to the cost of a new bridge, not to mention the benefits of preserving this priceless coastal treasure.[9] In 2005 it was listed on the National Register of Historic Places.

While the Yaquina Bay Bridge rightfully earned fame as the Oregon coast's centerpiece span, and into the 21st century Yaquina Bay and Newport still showcase the central coast's vibrancy in tourism and development, in the mid 19th century the Yaquina area was central to a much more deplorable circumstance.

Native Americans inhabited Oregon's coastal lands for thousands of years before Euro-Americans began to arrive in the late eighteenth century. The first historic record of a sighting of the Yaquina Bay area by non-Native Americans occurred on March 7, 1778, when English Captain James Cook, searching for the fabled Northwest Passage with two ships, the *Resolution* and

Ship's eye view as one passes under the deck of the bridge facing north.

Cathedral arches as seen from north bank of the Yaquina River facing south.

The center span arch of the bridge featuring the metal railings which replaced the concrete originals as seen from the deck facing north.

70

The Yaquina Bay Bridge's main 600-foot steel through arch is flanked on either side by a pair of decorative concrete pylons and 350-foot steel deck arch spans.

Discovery, logged a description of a rocky headland just north of Yaquina Bay. He named it "Cape Foulweather," a sobriquet that survives to the present day.[10] It wasn't until 1826 that Alexander McLeod, an explorer/trapper for the Hudson Bay Company, sighted the bay from land.[11]

While the name Yaquina Bay memorializes the native Oregonians who originally lived along its shores its development, as was common throughout the West, exacted a terrible toll on them. Diseases spread by the early seafarers, fur trappers, and miners swept through the native people in Oregon, killing most of them. By the time settlers began arriving from the Oregon Trail in the 1840s, Oregon's native people were facing extinction. Pressure mounted to remove Oregon's few surviving Native Americans from their homelands onto reservations. In 1855 the U.S. government created a large land preserve on a long, broad strip of mostly coastal land running from the Yamhill River on the north to the Siuslaw River on the south. It centered on Yaquina Bay, land then thought to be of little value. The remaining tribes in western Oregon were literally rounded up by federal troops and marched to the preserve.[12] In 1855-1856 this land was divided into two adjacent reservations: The Siletz along the coast, and the Grand Ronde in the northern interior section.

It was only a matter of time, of course, before the Euro-Americans began to see the potential value of the coastal reservation land. In the 1850s,

miners migrated up from California, hoping to strike it rich from gold deposits along the coast. Oyster beds, originally discovered in 1852, were rediscovered in the early 1860s, and a lucrative trade developed. Then, with improved transportation links, the coast began to be utilized as a recreational destination.[13]

Initially 4,000 Indians lived on the reservations. By 1868 the number had dropped to 2,500, and by 1892 only 500 remained. In 1954, the Grand Ronde Tribe was "terminated," which meant that the U.S. government no longer recognized the tribe or its people, and sold all but 7.5 acres of the tribe's land.[14] The Siletz suffered a similar fate, losing nearly all their land, then their tribal status. It finally regained tribal recognition as the Confederated Tribes of Siletz in 1977 and its reservation today consists of more than 3,600 acres.[15] In 1983, after a prolonged and dedicated effort by tribal members and their supporters, the U.S. government once again formally recognized the Grand Ronde Federated Tribes. In 1988, Congress re-established a 9,811-acre reservation in the mountains north of Grand Ronde.

After hanging on for 150 years, both the Siletz and Grand Ronde Confederated Tribes found an economic niche, when in 1995 the Siletz opened the Chinook Winds Casino and Resort, and in 1996 the Grand Ronde opened the wildly prosperous Spirit Mountain Casino and Resort that became one of Oregon's most extraordinary business success stories.[16]

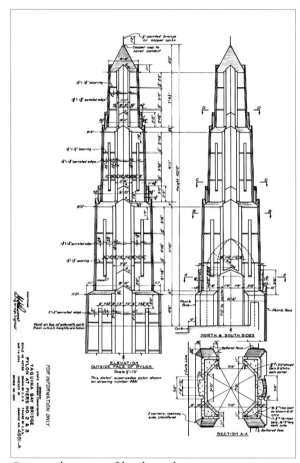
Design drawing of bridge pylon.

The name Newport came about in 1866 when Samuel Case, a military volunteer stationed in the area during the Civil War, and his associate, Dr. J.R. Bayley, built and operated the Ocean House on the north beach of Yaquina Bay where the U.S. Coast Guard building now stands. Case, originally from Maine, was familiar with Newport Beach, Rhode Island, where the first big hotel constructed there was named "Ocean House." Seeing the potential for a resort at Yaquina Bay, Case built his own hotel, naming it the Ocean House after the Eastern resort and the town after Newport Beach.[17]

Bridge as seen from the deck with its matching pylons.

Yaquina Bay Bridge as seen from the south jetty.

The Alsea Bay Bridge's towering steel and cable arch makes it one of the most impressive bridges built on the Oregon coast in recent history.

⑱ Alsea Bay (Waldport) Bridge
ARC DE TRIOMPHE

The new Alsea Bay Bridge opened to great fanfare on August 24, 1991, and for good reason. The first major bridge to be constructed along the coast in a quarter century (after the Columbia River Bridge in 1966), it bore the bittersweet fate of replacing an icon, the ill-fated original Alsea Bay Bridge constructed under the Oregon Coast Bridges Project (1934 to 1936), and widely considered to be the best of Conde B. McCullough's coastal masterpieces. Philip Parrish, in *Historic Oregon* (The Macmillan Co., 1943) echoed the opinion of many when he labeled it a "symphony in concrete."

While the new bridge lacks the stunning visual appeal of McCullough's brilliant original design, its towering steel and cable arch makes it the most impressive major bridge built in Oregon since Portland's Fremont Bridge over the Willamette River in 1973 and a welcome addition to the coast highway bridge collection.

Vaguely reminiscent of the original bridge's multi-arched grandeur, the new bridge's arch design represented a hard-won victory by preservationists and bridge enthusiasts. The initial groundswell of opposition to the proposed new bridge focused on saving the old one. In response, the Oregon Department of Transportation (ODOT) agreed to finance an independent assessment of the old bridge. It confirmed that it was too deteriorated to justify renovating it, sealing the old Alsea's fate.

Construction of the original Alsea Bay Bridge in 1935.

ALSEA BAY BRIDGE
Technical Data

Location: City of Waldport, Lincoln County; Oregon Coast Highway (US 101), Milepost 155.5

Year completed: 1991

Type: Steel through arch

Length: 2,910 feet

Deck to streambed: 70 feet

Description: From the north end there are two reinforced-concrete box girder spans of 195 and 264 feet, a 450-foot central steel arch (90 feet high) with reinforced-concrete box girder approaches of 236, 230, 225, 215, 205, 195, 155, 145, 140, 135, 120 feet; four traffic lanes, 6-foot shoulders, and two 6-foot walkways

Cost: $42.5 million

Contractor: General Construction Company, Seattle, Washington

Project manager: Phil Rabb

Designer: Howard Needles Tammen & Bergendoff, Bellevue, Washington

Ownership: State of Oregon

Underside of the original bridge.

The original Alsea Bay Bridge supported three arches on the deck and a matched set of three flanking arches below.

The original Alsea Bay Bridge being demolished with the newly constructed bridge in the background.

Once it became clear that a new bridge needed to be constructed, preservationists shifted their efforts to persuade ODOT to construct a more distinguished bridge than the proposed freeway-type span. ODOT responded by opening a design competition for the bridge, finally selecting the design submitted by Howard Needles Tammen & Bergendoff, of Bellevue, Washington.

The old bridge remained standing long enough to witness the opening of the new bridge in August 1991. According to press releases at the time, its stately presence cast a haunting shadow on the new bridge's opening, making the dedication ceremonies more a requiem for the old bridge than a celebration of the new one. Governor Barbara Roberts joked that she hesitated to call the historic bridge "old," since she was born the same year it was dedicated, and then observed that the "original bridge has served Oregon well, and we will be sorry to see it go."[1]

Congressional Representative Les AuCoin, noting that the arch design of the new bridge was the result of the efforts of preservationists and enthusiasts of the old bridge, praised the citizens of Waldport (and Oregon) for rejecting the flat, conventional bridge originally proposed by ODOT. "What you did was to settle for something better than second best," he said. "We're here today to dedicate a bridge that captures your spirit and the spirit of the history of Oregon."[2]

Eighty-one year old Al Johnson of Salem, a former deputy highway engineer who worked on the bridge as an inspector, attended the ceremony. He recalled taking a fall off the bridge and landing unhurt into the chilly waters of the bay. "I walked right off the end of a beam," he said. His take on the new bridge? It's a "very fine" structure. "But I hate to see the old one wrecked," he added, echoing the prevailing sentiment.[3]

It's never easy to replace a masterpiece, but without question the new bridge is impressive. Just over 3,000 feet long, it sits on huge Y-shaped piers and its single steel arch soars 170 feet above the bay.[4] The design makes use of modern technology and materials while trying to preserve some of the historic character of the old bridge. To prevent, or at least delay, the corrosive effects of the salt air on the steel reinforcing bar used in the bridge (the primary cause of the old bridge's demise), all reinforcing steel is coated with epoxy. Builders used latex concrete for the bridge's road deck

View of the new bridge looking south.

and insulated the steel in the piers behind four inches of concrete (rather than the normal one-inch layer) to protect it from the corrosive salt air. Whereas the old bridge was built on shallow timber piles that marine borer worms ate away over the years, the new bridge's steel and concrete piling reach down more than one hundred feet to bedrock. These improvements give the bridge a conservative life expectancy of a hundred years.

Designers also incorporated some of the entry pylons, spires, and railings from the old span into a viewpoint on the north end of the bridge. The Interpretive Center at the southwest end of the bridge provides information about the old bridge, early road

development, Native American history, and pioneer settlement in the area. The center also houses an impressive model of the original bridge constructed by James Yarger.

It's clear that the original Alsea Bay Bridge, perhaps Conde B. McCullough's most memorable design, has risen to the richly deserved, rarified realm of an Oregon icon.

According to *Oregon Geographic Names*, David Ruble founded the town of Waldport. The name apparently was the brainchild of the first postmaster P.V. Wustrow, when the post office was established in 1871. It combines the German word wald, meaning "forest," with the English word "port," an apt description for the area.

The Cape Perpetua Half Viaduct is a two-span reinforced-concrete deck girder structure.

Cape Perpetua Half Viaduct
MORE BY HALF

Cape Perpetua Half Viaduct, one of the smallest but most unique bridges profiled in this book, sits just a mile north of Cooks Chasm Bridge. The only span of its type on the coastal highway, it is a 76-foot, two-span reinforced-concrete deck girder structure (each span measuring 38 feet) that carries the highway around the sheer rocky cliff face of Cape Perpetua, two hundred feet above the ocean.

This bridge's unusual railing features a masonry guardrail with broad arched openings and a concrete cap. This bridge exhibits the only example of an open-arched masonry balustrade on a coastal bridge, likely the product of the Works Progress Administration, the Depression-era program that sponsored many similar projects around Oregon, including several along the coast. Many consider the bridge eligible for nomination on the National Register of Historic Places.

CAPE PERPETUA HALF VIADUCT
Technical Data

Location: Yachats vicinity, Lincoln County; Oregon Coast Highway (US 101), Milepost 166.5

Year completed: 1931

Length: 78 feet

Description: Two 38-foot. reinforced-concrete deck girders, masonry rail, 3.5-foot. sidewalks

Deck to streambed: 27 feet

Contractor: Tom Lillebo

Ownership: State of Oregon

Renovation contract: Cathodic protection system in 1989

Cooks Chasm Bridge, completed in 2003, has a reinforced-concrete deck arch with exposed and interlocking beams.

20

Cooks Chasm Bridge

ENGLISH MARINER'S SAINTLY LEGACY

A few miles south of Yachats, mighty Cape Perpetua juts boldly into the sea. English sea captain James Cook sighted this dramatic basaltic headland in 1778 and named it for Saint Perpetua, an early Christian convert martyred in Rome in AD 203.[1]

Long deep fissures, or chasms lie within the basalt contours of this outcropping land formation, into which the surf rolls and churns. The bridge spans one of the most picturesque of these and bears Cook's name.

Cook left no clue as to why he named the cape after Perpetua. Since he first sighted Oregon's shores on March 7, 1778, the date of St. Perpetua's martyrdom, perhaps he intended to commemorate the perpetual struggle he and his crew had faced. Or, if he took time to investigate the area, the mighty struggle between earth and tide at this site may have reminded him of Perpetua's struggle against overwhelming forces of a different kind.

This new reinforced-concrete deck arch, reminiscent of the McCullough era, brings a distinctive touch to the dramatic landscape surrounding it. While McCullough typically utilized the Art Deco motif fancied by his era, this bridge's ornamentation reflects more of the Craftsman style with its exposed and interlocking beams. The superficial arched railings are similar to McCullough touches utilized at Rocky Creek and Depoe Bay.

A nice viewing area now adjoins the north approach, allowing visitors to watch the action of the surf as it charges through the chasm below. Like its new friend down the coast, the Brush Creek Bridge, it reflects the current mindset of the Oregon Department of Transportation's Bridge Engineering Section to bring quality design to all new Oregon bridges. The new bridge, completed in 2003, replaced a simple reinforced-concrete girder span built in 1931 that reflected its era. But, after sixty years of service, it showed significant signs of deterioration.

The area around Cape Perpetua deserves some exploring. Visit the Cape Perpetua Scenic Area Interpretive Center located just north of the bridge for outstanding views, cultural and natural histories of the area, a gift/book shop and theater, nature walks, and trailheads to more than twenty-five miles of hiking trails accessing old-growth forest, tide pools, and beaches.

Original 1931 reinforced-concrete girder span bridge.

83

COOKS CHASM BRIDGE
Technical Data

Location: Yachats vicinity, Lincoln County; Oregon Coast Highway (US 101), Milepost 167.5

Year completed: 2003

Type: Reinforced-concrete deck arch

Bridge length: 175 feet

Deck arch: 126 feet

Deck to streambed: 57 feet

Description: One 126-foot reinforced-concrete deck arch flanked by two 24-foot, 7-inch reinforced-concrete slab approaches and 5-foot sidewalks

Contractor: F.E. Ward Inc., Vancouver, Washington

Ownership: State of Oregon

Detail of railings, stonework and arch supports.

Bridge as viewed from the south looking north.

Cummins Creek Bridge is a reinforced-concrete deck arch bridge designed by Conde B. McCullough.

21

Cummins Creek Bridge
GRACEFUL GEM

Just south of Cape Perpetua and Cooks Chasm Bridge sits Cummins Creek Bridge, an appealing but often overlooked reinforced-concrete deck arch bridge designed by Conde B. McCullough. One of his smallest and least-known bridges, it spans the creek named for F.L. Cummins, an early homesteader in the area.[1] Located within Neptune State Park, one of dozens of scenic and convenient state roadside parks that dot the Oregon Coast Highway and provide access to the beach, the bridge contributes to an attractive package well worth the visit.

From the park's ocean edge, visitors can walk along the creek bed of rounded stones and catch a full view of the bridge's graceful low-rise open-spandrel arch. Geometric lines scored into the concrete surface add interest to the bridge's façade, creating the illusion that it is constructed of stone blocks. The Rogue River Bridge, one of McCullough's most famous bridges and constructed about the same time, also features this technique. The flutings on the main piers, spandrel columns, and railing posts are common McCullough touches, as are the round arch openings of the railing supports.[2]

There has been some speculation that Cummins Creek Bridge was not designed by McCullough. Apparently its history is clouded by a lack of documentation. I believe, however, that the bridge's broad graceful arch and its carefully executed surface details typify many of McCullough's reinforced-concrete coastal arch bridges. *Historic Highway Bridges of Oregon* also attributes the bridge to McCullough. Let's say the preponderance of evidence leans in McCullough's favor. But his or not, the bridge and beautiful site make it a required stop for bridge lovers.

Underside of bridge.

CUMMINS CREEK BRIDGE
Technical Data

Location: Yachats vicinity, Lincoln County; Oregon Coast Highway (US 101), Milepost 167.5

Year completed: 1931

Type: Reinforced-concrete deck arch

Bridge length: 175 feet

Deck arch: 126 feet

Deck to streambed: 57 feet

Description: One 126-foot reinforced-concrete deck arch flanked by two 24-foot, 7-inch reinforced-concrete slab approaches and 5-foot sidewalks

Designer: Conde B. McCullough

Contractor: F.E. Ward Inc., Vancouver, Washington

Ownership: State of Oregon

Renovation contract: Cathodic protection system in 2001

Bridge viewed looking north.

BUTTERFLY RESCUED TIED-ARCH TWINS

Along a gorgeous, grassy stretch of highway tracing the ocean shore a few miles south of Yachats sits a pair of nearly identical reinforced-concrete arch bridges—Tenmile Creek Bridge and its southern neighbor, Big Creek Bridge. These bridges, whose central 120-foot arches are identical to the Wilson River Bridge near Tillamook, share the distinction of being among the first tied-arch bridges in the Northwest. (For a more detailed description of the tied arch, see the Wilson River Bridge.) Though simple in design, these single-arch spans grace their respective sites in a most alluring way, providing an unexpected visual pleasure while traveling along the coast.

Tenmile Creek Bridge, a reinforced-concrete through tied-arch bridge, is located near Stonefield Beach State Wayside.

22

Tenmile Creek Bridge

BUTTERFLY RESCUED TIED-ARCH TWIN

According to *Oregon Geographic Names*, Tenmile Creek bears the ignominy of being named by surveyors simply for the distance from its source to the sea. The more northern of the tied-arch twins, Tenmile Creek benefited from Big Creek Bridge's butterfly protection environmental windfall. With reserve funds from the Big Creek Bridge restoration, modifications of the wind-bracing members were made on Tenmile Creek Bridge.

Tenmile Creek bridge before cathodic protection system was installed.

TENMILE CREEK BRIDGE

Technical Data

Location: Six miles south of Yachats, Lane County; Oregon Coast Highway (US 101), Milepost 171.4

Year completed: 1931

Type: Reinforced-concrete through tied arch

Length: 180 feet; 120-foot main span

Deck to streambed: 18 feet

Description: One 30-foot reinforced-concrete deck girder span, one 120-foot reinforced-concrete through tied arch, one 30-foot reinforced-concrete deck girder span, two 7-foot sidewalks

Designer: Conde B. McCullough

Contractor: Union Bridge Company

Ownership: State of Oregon

Renovation contract: Cathodic protection system installed in 2007

Big Creek Bridge was preserved in order to save the Oregon silverspot butterfly.

Big Creek Bridge

BUTTERFLY RESCUED TIED-ARCH TWIN

At 235 feet in length, Big Creek Bridge bears the distinction of being the longest of the three identical tied arches, save for the approach spans. Its overall greater length results from dual 40-foot reinforced-concrete deck girder spans adjoining the 120-foot central arch to the north and a 35-foot deck girder span to the south. All three bridges incorporate decorative precast arched concrete railings.

Like many of the older reinforced-concrete bridges along the coast, Big Creek Bridge displayed significant deterioration after seventy years of exposure to the salty marine environment. Highway officials evaluated various options and recommended replacing the bridge. At the last moment, however, this historic bridge found a friend in—of all things—a butterfly! It was determined that to construct a temporary bridge while the old bridge was being replaced threatened to destroy critical habitat of the Oregon silverspot butterfly. Rather than fight a complicated environmental battle, the Oregon Department of Transportation, U.S. Fish and Wildlife Service, and Federal Highway Administration agreed on a plan to rehabilitate the old bridge.[1]

The extensive rehabilitation included repairing all concrete and metal structural members, installing a cathodic protection system to retard steel corrosion in the bridge, and modifying the "X" wind-bracing members at each end of the bridge to "Lazy Ks" to improve the vertical clearance for traffic.[2]

Because of Big Creek Bridge's eligibility for listing on the National Register of Historic Places, the rehabilitation preserved both the historic value and structural integrity of the bridge.

BIG CREEK BRIDGE

Technical Data

Location: Oregon Coast Highway (US 101) Milepost 175

Year completed: 1931

Type: Reinforced-concrete through tied arch

Length: 235 feet; 120-foot main span

Deck to streambed: 21 feet

Description: Two 40-foot reinforced-concrete deck girder spans, one 120-foot reinforced-concrete through tied arch, one 35-foot reinforced-concrete deck girder span, two 5-foot sidewalks outside the arches

Designer: Conde B. McCullough

Contractor: Union Bridge Company

Ownership: State of Oregon

Renovation contract: Cathodic protection system in 1998

Cape Creek Bridge, a double-tiered viaduct and concrete deck arch is one of Conde B. McCullough's most unique bridges.

Cape Creek Bridge
ROMAN REFLECTION

Cape Creek Bridge, located 12 miles north of Florence, stands near one of the coast's most famous landmarks, Heceta Head Lighthouse. Named after Spanish mariner Bruno de Hezeta, who first mapped the point in 1775, Heceta Head juts into the sea just north of another promontory known as Devil's Elbow. Splitting these two headlands, picturesque Cape Creek runs its last few miles between the fern-lined banks of a beautiful cottonwood stand before rippling silently under Cape Creek Bridge into the ocean.

One of Conde B. McCullough's most unique bridges, Cape Creek Bridge spans the gorge between these two major promontories. The double-tiered viaduct and concrete deck arch became an integral part of one of the most difficult and costly construction projects on the coast highway, dubbed the "Million-Dollar Mile."[1] Constructing the "mile" required carving a shelf for the highway out of sheer rock cliffs hundreds of feet above the surf, blasting a 700-foot tunnel through Devil's Elbow, and finally, constructing a bridge connecting the tunnel's northern end to Heceta Head. (Devil's Elbow tunnel is one of two tunnels along the coast highway; the other is at Arch Cape.)

The bridge's splendor can best be viewed from Devil's Elbow State Park below, which is accessed from the north end of the bridge. This cloistered little beach provides excellent views of the bridge and is a favorite picnic and wading site of Oregon coast devotees. Sea lions, part of the clan that inhabits the nearby Sea Lion Caves, can often be seen lazing on the rocks at the north end.

The only bridge of its kind in Oregon, the deck arch clearly reflects the design of Roman viaducts and aqueducts like the famous Pont du Gard near Nimes, France. The interplay between the rhythmic pattern of the stout lower arches, the road-bearing higher arches, and the graceful central arch make this classically inspired bridge in its beautiful setting one of the most unusual and pleasing visual experiences along the coast highway.

Its distinct style also has purpose, as bridging this lovely gorge required unusual engineering techniques. Typically, rubble fill would have been used as approaches to the arched reinforced-concrete span, but here the steep slopes on either end would have required huge amounts of fill that might have been threatened by the unstable land formations beneath the bridge site and severely impacted the beautiful site below. To address these concerns, and after many design considerations, McCullough finally opted for the two-tiered viaduct structure.[2] Thirty faux-arched sections spanning the entire gorge make up the upper level, supported by the lower level that features a 220-foot open-spandrel reinforced-concrete deck arch rising 104 feet above the creek, flanked by seven arched sections on the north and three on the south.

Concerns about the stability of the terrain were validated when, shortly after the bridge's completion in 1931, sub-strata settling and lateral shifting caused cracking on the bridge's sides. The cracks were repaired

CAPE CREEK BRIDGE
Technical Data

Location: Heceta Head, Lane County; Oregon Coast Highway (US 101), Milepost 178.3

Year completed: 1931

Type: Reinforced-concrete deck arch

Length: 619 feet; main arch 220 feet

Deck to streambed: 104 feet

Description: Double-tiered reinforced-concrete deck arch; one 30-foot, one 20-foot, six 40-foot reinforced-concrete spans on concrete columns; one 200-foot open-spandrel rib-type reinforced-concrete deck arch; one 40-foot, one 41-foot, and one 28-foot reinforced-concrete span; two 3.5-foot sidewalks

Designer: Conde B. McCullough

Contractor: John K. Holt, main arch; Clackamas Construction Co., north viaduct

Cost: $187,434

Ownership: State of Oregon

Renovation contract: Cathodic protection system installed in 1989

Bridge during construction.

The deck arch clearly reflects the design of Roman viaducts and aqueducts.

and the bridge required little attention until the late 1960s. Later, maintenance engineers discovered that reinforcing bar was corroding, a common problem for many of the McCullough-era reinforced-concrete bridges, including the Alsea and Yaquina bridges, whose repairs took priority over those of Cape Creek.[3]

Finally, in 1984 the Stauch Construction Company of Grants Pass contracted to repair Cape Creek's rocker joints that had frozen from salt corrosion. In 1989 the Oregon Department of Transportation installed a cathodic protection system like those used on the Alsea Bay and Yaquina Bay bridges.[4]

These efforts to preserve the Cape Creek Bridge have mostly been successful, but careful maintenance must be continued for this beautiful bridge to survive.

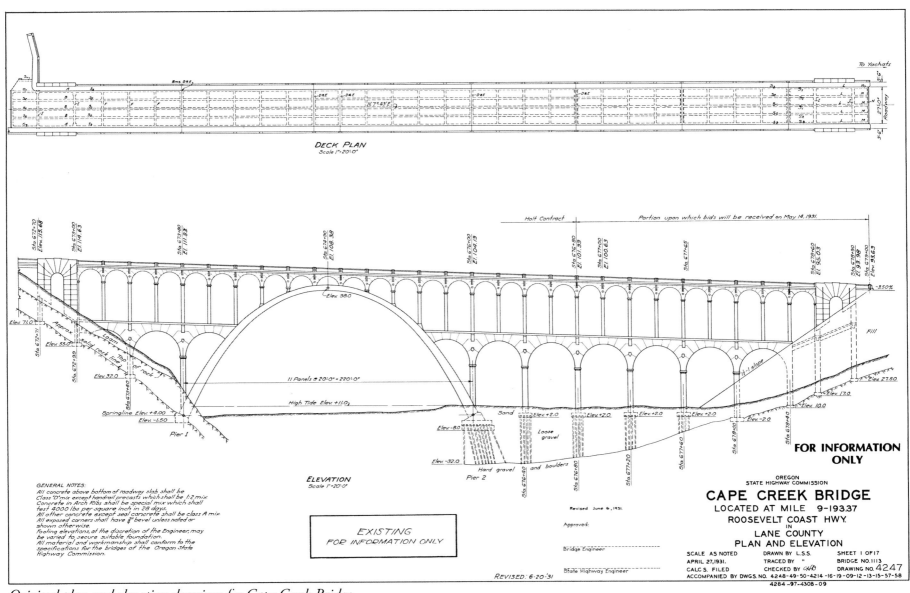

Original plan and elevation drawings for Cape Creek Bridge.

Historic photo of the bridge viewed looking west.

The Siuslaw River drawbridge is the most ornate of McCullough's major coastal bridges.

Siuslaw River (Florence) Bridge

DECO-GOTHIC DRAWBRIDGE

The Siuslaw River Bridge, the smallest and least expensive of the five Great Depression-era bridges constructed under the Oregon Coast Bridges Project, connects the towns of Florence and Glenada. It became the first to open on March 31, 1936, although the formal dedication was postponed until May 23 and 24. Of the five-bridge group, it is the only drawbridge. Designer Conde B. McCullough explained that "the topography of the surrounding country is such that it was not practicable to place a structure high enough to clear water craft using this river, therefore a drawbridge has been built."[1]

Interestingly, this unique drawbridge is a composite of components that McCullough used on other coastal bridges. He no doubt drew from the design of his earlier Old Youngs Bay drawbridge near Astoria in creating this steel double-leaf central bascule span, which consists of two 70-foot central cantilevered sections. The narrow, deep channel lends itself to a double-leaf bascule. It is flanked by two reinforced-concrete through-tied arches of 154 feet, identical to the ones that flanked the central span of the original Alsea Bay Bridge and the Umpqua River Bridge. The draw span is raised by two 15-horsepower electric motors like those used on the Umpqua River Bridge. When open, it provides a clear horizontal distance of 140 feet between piers. As with the Umpqua, safeguards built into the draw mechanism require the roadway gates to be closed before the leaves of the bridge will open.

The most ornate of McCullough's major coastal bridges, the need for a drawbridge likely influenced the architectural theme reminiscent of a turreted medieval castle. Gothic-inspired Art Deco pylons flank both entrances of the concrete arches and, at each corner of the central draw span, large Gothic-arched concrete guardhouses with pointed spires at the crown "protect" the drawbridge. Their only purpose here, however, besides decoration, is to guard the drawbridge controls and provide some storage.

Like most of the larger communities along the coast, Florence was originally a river town whose business center fronted the Siuslaw's northern bank. On the western end of Bay Street, at what is now a mini-park, motorists lined up to take the ferry. The bridge, completed in 1936, connected Florence with Glenada along an elevated US101 that literally passed over the heart of Florence and the ferry landing, and a new "strip town" developed along the highway. For decades, old Florence languished, an abandoned relic of an earlier era. Restoration efforts revived the old town, however, and today one can stroll through a new Old Florence with the river and bridge as a backdrop and get a feel for what Florence was like as a river town before the highway and bridge changed it forever.

The town of Florence, situated at the northern end of what is now the Oregon Dunes National Recreation Area, incorporated in 1893. The derivation of its name is uncertain. As local lore would have it, the town was named after a French sailing ship that wrecked on the Siuslaw River bar in 1875. According to Lewis A. McArthur's *Oregon Geographic Names*, however, the town was likely named after A.B. Florence, a member of the Oregon State Senate who represented Lane County from 1858 to 1860.[2]

SIUSLAW RIVER BRIDGE
Technical Data

Location: Florence, Lane County; Oregon Coast Highway (US 101), Milepost 190.9

Year completed: 1936

Type: Steel double-leaf bascule draw span

Length: 1,568 feet

Deck to streambed: 70 feet

Description: One 56-foot, one 70-foot, four 56-foot, one 70-foot, one 56-foot reinforced-concrete deck girder span; one 154-foot reinforced-concrete through tied arch; one 300-ton, 140-foot double-leaf bascule draw span; one 154-foot reinforced-concrete through tied arch; one 56-foot, one 70-foot, two 56-foot, one 70-foot, one 56-foot, one 42-foot, one 56-foot, and one 42-foot reinforced-concrete deck girder spans; a 27-foot wide roadway; two 3.5-foot sidewalks

Designer: Conde B. McCullough

Bridge engineer: Conde B. McCullough

Resident engineer: Arthur Jordan

Contractor: Mercer-Fraser, Eureka, California; H.E. Acheson, Superintendent

Cost: $527,069

Ownership: State of Oregon

The bridge during its construction in 1935.

Historic view of the completed bridge.

View from the deck of the bridge in 1936.

Bull gear and trunnion.

Close-up view of Gothic-arched concrete guardhouse.

104

Smith River Bridge, Bolon Cut, and Umpqua River Bridge

THREE IN ONE

Spanning two rivers here required three separate projects: The Umpqua River Bridge, the primary project, crosses the Umpqua's southern channel, connecting Reedsport with Bolon Island. The second project, a 140-foot cut through Bolon Island, carries traffic to the Smith River Bridge, the final project, which connects with the northern mainland.

The Smith River Bridge is a reinforced-concrete deck girder span.

Smith River Bridge

JEDEDIAH SMITH MEMORIAL

The Smith River, named for Jedediah Smith, the intrepid and early Oregon explorer and fur trader, flows into the Umpqua just east of the Smith River Bridge and still carries his name as it flows through the channel on the north side of Bolon Island. Though constructed as part of the Umpqua River Bridge crossing that was funded under the five-bridge Oregon Coast Bridges Project, both the Smith River Bridge and the Bolon Cut were state projects financed by separate federal funding.[1]

The original Smith River Bridge, an unusual curved 1,600-foot wooden pile trestle, connected Bolon Island with the northern mainland. Simple, yet durable, it survived for 63 years before being replaced in 1999 with a reinforced-concrete deck girder structure, almost identical in shape and size to the original span.

Bolon Island, the craggy tip of a 10,000-foot deep sandstone deposit created 40 to 60 million years ago during the Eocene Period and named for an early settler,[3] became both a blessing and a curse for the bridge builders. While it provided a natural abutment for the north end of the main bridge, when setting the bridge piers engineers discovered that over time great slabs of rock had broken off the island and fallen into the river. These slabs were not large enough to support the piers but were too large to drive piling through them. Finally, holes had to be drilled and filled with dynamite and the rock slabs blasted out of the way in order to reach bedrock.[2]

In 1828 Smith and his party of seventeen men camped near this site after a strenuous six-month trek from California. We know from Smith's diaries that following an altercation with local Indians, Smith and two of his men left camp to scout the area. Returning a few hours later, they found the entire remaining party dead at the hand of the Indians. Smith and his two companions fled on foot to Fort Vancouver where, to their surprise, they found another of their comrades who had also escaped the attack.[3]

SMITH RIVER BRIDGE
Technical Data

Location: Reedsport, Douglas County; Oregon Coast Highway (US 101), Milepost 210.5

Type: Reinforced-concrete deck girder

Year completed: 1999

Length: 1,640 feet

Deck to streambed: 12 feet

Description: Twelve 118-foot reinforced-concrete deck girders flanked by two 111-foot, 6-inch reinforced-concrete deck girder approach

Ownership: State of Oregon

BOLON ISLAND CUT SECTION

Excavation contracts: Haskin & Brooks; E.C. Hall

Cost: $200,423

Ownership: State of Oregon

The Umpqua River Bridge's steel-through truss span is the largest swing span in Oregon.

Umpqua River (Reedsport) Bridge
ANCIENT ANTECEDENTS

The Umpqua River Bridge located just north of Reedsport, one of the five major bridges designed by Conde B. McCullough and constructed under the Oregon Coast Bridges Project, became the second movable bridge of the group. Least picturesque of the five bridges, but still an excellent example of McCullough's bridge engineering skills, the Umpqua employs a central swing span similar to one he earlier designed for the Coquille River Bridge in 1922 (not to be confused with the US 101 Coquille River Bridge), where the bridge needed to cross a wide, shallow channel. His often-used 154-foot tied-arch approach spans, identical to those on the Siuslaw River Bridge and the original Alsea Bay Bridge, are also used here as paired twins flanking the center span.[1]

Designed to accommodate river traffic at that time, the Umpqua's 430-foot steel-through truss span remains the largest swing span in Oregon. When open for river traffic, it provides two 182-foot navigation channels. Similar to the Siuslaw River Bridge, the swing span comes equipped with interlocking safety mechanisms operated by two 60-horsepower electric controllers, one in the operating house above the roadway and the other in a panel alongside the sidewalk.

The 430-foot central swing span is flanked left and right by two 154-foot bridge spans.

UMPQUA RIVER BRIDGE
Technical Data

Location: Reedsport, Douglas County; Oregon Coast Highway (US 101), Milepost 211.1

Year completed: 1936

Type: Steel through truss (Parker) swing

Length: 2,206 feet

Deck to streambed: 12 feet

Description: One 430-foot structural steel swing draw span flanked by four 154-foot reinforced-concrete arches; a 1,160-foot concrete viaduct connects to the south approach. The span is 27 feet wide at the roadway with 3.5-foot pedestrian walkways.

Bridge designer: Conde B. McCullough

Resident engineers: Dexter R. Smith and L.L. Jensen

Contractor: Teufel and Carlson, Seattle, Washington; L. G. Murray, Superintendent

Cost: $551,234

Ownership: State of Oregon

Detail of bridge trusswork.

View of the Umpqua River Bridge in 1935 during construction.

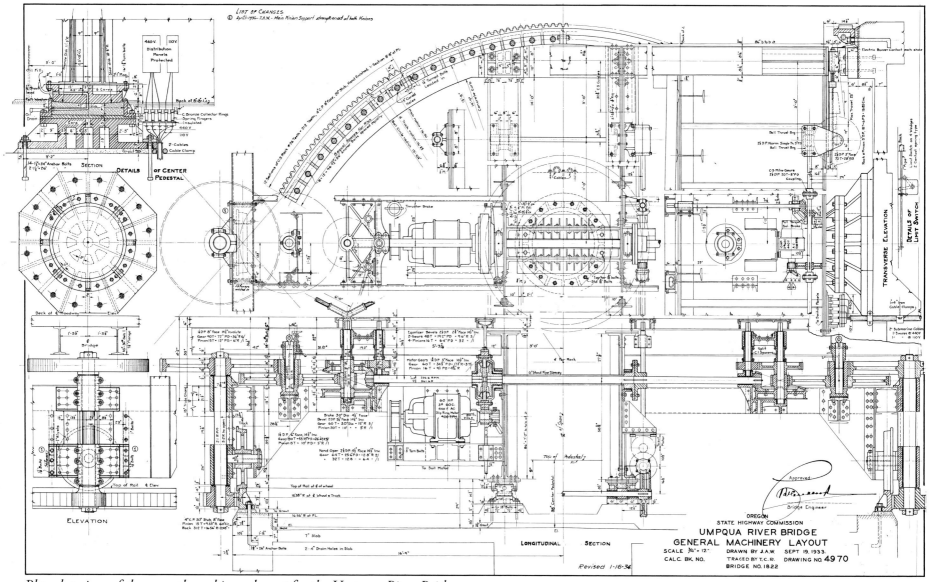

Plan drawings of the general machinery layout for the Umpqua River Bridge.

The dramatic growth in vehicular traffic along the Oregon Coast Highway, coupled with the concomitant decline in river traffic, leaves movable bridges like the Umpqua all but obsolete. It is one of only five remaining swing spans in the Oregon State Highway System. Though rarely used now, the Umpqua's swing span remains an important example of McCullough's engineering skill and a valuable piece of the Oregon Coast Highway's bridge heritage

An ancient Oregon river, according to *Oregon Geographic Names*, Umpqua was an Indian name used to describe the general locality around the river. The river received its current name in 1825 from David Douglas, the British horticulturalist who traveled through the area, and for whom the Douglas Fir is named.[2]

Northbound view of bridge deck.

The Haynes Inlet Slough Bridge as viewed from the northwest riverbank.

Haynes Inlet Slough Bridge

OYSTER PEARL

Haynes Inlet Slough Bridge, a modest antecedent to the majestic Coos Bay Bridge for visitors traveling from the north, personifies one of the new breed of coastal highway bridges. It combines attractive two-hinged concrete deck arches with 120-year construction methods that include stainless steel reinforcement bar and cathodic protection. This bridge replaced a 1953 reinforced-concrete deck girder bridge constructed on timber pile trestles.

According to *Oregon Geographic Names* and *Dodge's Pioneer History of Coos and Curry Counties*, the inlet was named for Henry Haines, an early settler who discovered coal near the present site of Glasgow, just south of the inlet. Somehow the name got misspelled and it remains Haynes to all recent mapmakers and highway sign painters.

Haynes Inlet is home to some of Oregon's best oyster beds, most notably Clausen Oysters, one of Oregon's largest oyster growers.

HAYNES INLET SLOUGH BRIDGE

Technical Data

Location: Coos County, North Bend vicinity; Oregon Coast Highway (US 101), Milepost 233.09

Constructed: 2001

Length: 775 feet

Arches: 60.35 feet

Contractors: Hamilton Construction Company

Designer: James Bollman

Cost: $12,500,000

The Coos Bay Bridge is considered by many to be Conde B. McCullough's crowning achievement.

Coos Bay (Conde B. McCullough) Bridge
McCULLOUGH MEMORIAL

M any people regard Conde B. McCullough's largest bridge, the gigantic yet graceful steel cantilever span over Coos Bay, as one of his finest achievements. Acknowledging his mastery of bridge design, in a rare tribute to a bridge engineer, the Coos Bay Bridge was posthumously dedicated to McCullough in 1947.

A plaque affixed to the bridge's entry reads:

MCCULLOUGH BRIDGE

DEDICATED TO THE MEMORY

OF

CONDE B. MCCULLOUGH

WHOSE GENIUS AND INSPIRATION ARE

MANIFEST IN THE DESIGN OF THIS

BRIDGE AND MANY OTHER OREGON

BRIDGES DURING HIS PERIOD OF

SERVICE AS BRIDGE ENGINEER

AND ASSISTANT STATE HIGHWAY

ENGINEER, 1919 TO 1946.

At slightly more than a mile in length, it is the last, longest, and most costly of the five bridges funded under the Oregon Coast Bridges Project during the Great Depression of the 1930s. For more than a quarter century it remained the coast highway's longest bridge until the completion of the Columbia River Bridge in 1966.

Coos Bay is Oregon's second largest shipping port, making it imperative that the bridge clear the shipping lanes without a draw span. This required the bridge to be of sufficient loft and span to allow ships to pass beneath, a task made easier by the great width of the bay and the high approaches at both ends. Regarding his choice of bridge, McCullough explained:

At Coos Bay, the central span demanded by navigation amounted to about 800 feet, which narrowed the choice to that between a cantilever and a self-anchored suspension type. The cantilever was finally chosen, although the cost of this type did not differ materially from that for the suspension type. In the selection of the chord outline and the employment of interior bracing, every attempt was made to render the structure architecturally harmonious.[1]

The "chord outline" refers to the use of curved top and bottom steel members of the cantilever span, an unusual feature employed not only

COOS BAY BRIDGE
Technical Data

Location: North Bend, Coos County; Oregon Coast Highway (US 101), M.P. 234.0

Year completed: 1936

Type: Steel through truss (cantilever)

Length: 5,305 feet

Deck to streambed: 180 feet

Description: This structure has a 1,708-foot through truss, with a main span of 793 feet and two anchor spans of 457.5 feet each, flanked by thirteen open spandrel, rib-type reinforced-concrete deck arches and concrete viaducts that connect to the mainland; the roadway is 27 feet wide with sidewalks 3.5 feet wide

Decorative features: Steel spires at portals to cantilever span; Gothic arch motif with transverse bracing of steel truss members

Designer: Conde B. McCullough

Engineers: Raymond Archibald, Dexter R. Smith

Contractor: Northwest Roads Company: concrete piers, arches, and viaducts; Virginia Bridge and Iron: furnishing and erecting the steel portion of the structure

Cost: $778,260

Ownership: State of Oregon

as a practical measure to give maximum shipping clearance, but also for design considerations. The "architecturally harmonious" quality was achieved by matching the rhythms of the concrete deck arch approaches with the arched chords of the central span. The "interior bracing" refers to the steel supports that form a series of Gothic arches above the roadway, creating an almost cathedral-like atmosphere as one passes "through" the bridge, beneath the truss work.

The suspension alternatives McCullough contemplated for spanning Coos Bay provide some interesting sources for speculation. Examples of McCullough suspension bridges, designed and constructed shortly after he designed the Coos Bay Bridge, were built in Guatemala, Honduras, and Panama. It's very likely that some of his preliminary designs for Coos Bay became realities in Central America.[2]

Strange as it may seem now, some consideration was given to using wood to construct the Coos Bay Bridge. With lumber from Oregon's forests so near and abundant, the timber lobby pressured McCullough to construct the Coos Bay and other coastal bridges of wood. While it's doubtful that McCullough ever seriously considered this alternative, he did draw some tentative designs and prepared cost estimates for a timber bridge. The cost of a wood bridge was estimated to be 30 to 40 percent cheaper than steel and concrete to build, but maintenance costs would surely have been significantly higher.[3]

Although steel and concrete trumped wood, the lumber needed to build the support structures for the concrete approach arches was nearly the amount required to construct a wooden bridge, which placated timber producers. The Coos Bay Bridge used approximately five million board feet of lumber. According to the *Coos Bay Times*, put on a single train averaging 120 cars per mile, such a train would be 25 miles long![4]

A cantilever truss 793 feet in length and rising to a maximum height of 180 feet above the water makes up the main span of the Coos Bay Bridge that crosses the shipping channel. The truss, balanced by anchor spans each 457.5 feet long, make the total length of steel construction 1,708 feet. The main towers supporting the bridge rise to a height of 280 feet above the water.

From an engineering point of view, structural components unseen below the water may be even more impressive than the beautiful structure seen

Construction of the bridge.

above. Before the bridge was even designed, state engineers bored test holes in Coos Bay to test the subsoil. Soil samples were taken more than 83 feet below the main pier on the north end, but they found no bedrock. Other tests as deep as 76 feet found only sand. Only one test found bedrock, but it was not in a position to do any good. This meant that the bridge would rest on piling.

To support the massive structure, 608 wooden piles were driven into the sandy bottom of the bay beneath each of the two main piers. In all, the bridge required 217,000 linear feet of piling. Each pile was driven 35 feet beyond what is called the "seal," a point 36 feet below water level where water can't reach it. At this depth, engineers claim, the piling would last indefinitely, even though they were untreated.

To drive the piling, cofferdams were constructed around the site to wall off the water before water inside the dam was pumped out. All the major bridges except the Siuslaw used steel sheet piling. In the Coos Bay Bridge, sheet piling used in the cofferdams rusted together, so divers used welding torches to cut and remove them. Once the piling was in place, the concrete poured on top of them created the piers upon which the bridge rests.[5]

A series of reinforced-concrete deck arches flank the steel center span, a common feature of McCullough's large coastal bridges. These arches gradually slope down to the approach embankments at either end of the bridge. The seven arches on the north end decrease from 265 feet to 151 feet in length; the six on the south

end from 265 feet to 171 feet. Viaducts connect the bridge with the mainland, where plazas built at each end include elaborate stairways descending into parks. These decorative yet utilitarian embellishments exemplify McCullough's major coastal bridges, and the southern approach of the Coos Bay Bridge became one of the most extravagant examples.

The approach lands within a 28-acre park donated to the state by Louis J. Simpson in memory of his father Asa Meade Simpson. Asa Simpson, generally considered to be North Bend's founder, amassed a fortune in lumber and shipping along the West Coast. Louis Simpson expanded the family fortune through land speculation and served as an early mayor of North Bend. He chaired the bridge's grand opening celebration committee.

Although the stairs are rarely used now, at the time the bridge was constructed, pedestrian traffic was heavier and the stairways provided access on and off the bridge. However, the fluid lines that integrate the stairways and plazas into the approaches did much more. Surrounded by parks, the design of these adornments softened the massive approaches of the structure and assimilated them into the landscape.

These beautifully designed entrances, especially the park setting at the southern end, reveal an important aspect of McCullough. Raised in horse and buggy days when people moved at a more leisurely pace, he envisioned people being drawn to his bridges as they are drawn to monuments everywhere. As a result he created public spaces for their pleasure and recreation. McCullough never anticipated that the pattern of automobile use would soon change the way

Construction of bridge pier.

bridge represented for local communities. In its Bridge Jubilee Edition, the banner headline of the *Coos Bay Times* read:

WEEK END BRINGS GALA BRIDGE CELEBRATION

QUEEN CHERRY I ASSUMES REIGN OVER FESTIVE COURT

To open the festivities on Friday morning, Governor Charles H. Martin crowned North Bend High School student Cherry Golder as Celebration Queen. Following the coronation, the queen and her court presided over a parade through North Bend that included a Pet Parade and Baby Parade with money prizes for all participant categories.

Queen Cherry and her court visited shut-ins at local hospitals. Boys and girls took part in running races. The Queen's Banquet and Ball capped Friday evening, officially lasting until 1:00 AM Saturday.

The formal dedication ceremonies for the bridge finally took place on Saturday afternoon, after a Marine Parade and boat races with $20 prizes for winners. Queen Cherry and her prime minister, Governor Martin, held court with the Queen's Privy Council, dignitaries that included local politicians and engineers responsible for designing and building the Coos Bay Bridge. After a brief message, Governor Martin pressed an electric button that dropped a barrier of silken ribbon allowing

people traveled and that speed and comfort in reaching destinations would become more important than relaxing scenic drives. This traffic battle still continues along the coast today, where the two-lane highway can be a frustrating experience if you're in a hurry but perfectly satisfactory for a leisurely sightseeing trip.

The bridge's opening ceremonies spanned three days, an indication of the importance the

The bridge takes form in this construction photo circa 1935.

South portal of bridge looking north.

a long string of cars to drive north across the bridge. Later that day the crowd watched another parade dedicated to transportation and industry, followed by a log bucking contest, another banquet, aerial fireworks, and a Mardi Gras Ball.

Sunday featured a trap shoot at the airport and various religious services, with sightseeing and pleasure trips in the afternoon to conclude the festivities.[6] The extraordinary three-day celebration helps us understand how important this beautiful bridge was to the residents of the

southern coast who had been isolated from the rest of Oregon for so long.

While the new bridge excited the local residents, some noted that the bridge also ended nearly twenty-five years of ferry service between North Bend and Glasgow.

View of the bridge from the southwest.

122

Detail view of central span tower, pier and truss.

(Note that the south end of the Coos Bay Bridge lands in North Bend, not Coos Bay [originally Marshfield].) The original ferry, built by Kruse and Banks at their North Bend shipyard, carried eighteen cars. Christened the *Roosevelt* by County Commissioner Henry Kern's daughter Lucille on July 21, 1921, its inaugural voyage was postponed until Saturday evening on May 6, 1922, because of problems installing the engine and boiler. In 1929 the larger *Oregon* (36 cars) was put into service and the *Roosevelt* became a backup when the *Oregon* was out of service or a supplement when traffic was heavy. At its busiest, the *Oregon* made four crossings an hour carrying more than 45,000 cars a month.[7]

The bridge suffered several minor collisions with ships, but one jolt in 1986 required closing the bridge for several weeks. Traveling at about nine knots, the Swedish freighter *Elgaren* entered the bay to load lumber when a loading ramp extending above the ship's stern struck the underside of the center span, causing some serious damage to two lower steel chords that provide the required tension and compression to keep the bridge's suspension span in place. After successful repair of the damaged parts, the bridge was judged good as new.[8]

The Coquille River Bridge is one of only two steel vertical lift spans along the Oregon Coast.

Coquille River (Bullards) Bridge

BULLARDS "GRAVE" BRIDGE

30

S panning the Coquille River just north of Bandon, the Coquille River Bridge, known locally as Bullards Bridge, takes its name from Bullards Ferry that once operated there. It is one of only two steel vertical lift spans along the Oregon Coast. Although the lift is rarely used now, since commercial river traffic between Bandon and Coquille has virtually disappeared, it can be raised with a 24-hour notice to the Oregon Department of Transportation.

Like its partner to the north, Youngs Bay Bridge at Astoria, the Coquille's utilitarian design displays little visual pretense. Nonetheless, after more than fifty years of service, its versatility and historic status as a period-piece bridge likely never to be built again warrants a well-deserved veneration. The bridge also stands as the most prominent remaining monument for a unique and nearly forgotten Oregon historical site, the little town of Bullards, whose development and demise are linked to this Coquille River crossing.

People have always been drawn to the area around Bullards. Archeological excavations reveal that the mouth of the Coquille River became a gathering place for Native Americans long before the arrival of Euro-Americans. Recent digs unearthed early Indian house pits dating from AD 500 to 1856.[1] By the latter date, California Gold Rush miners looking for new opportunities arrived to seek their fortunes in the gold-laden dunes of Whiskey Run just north of Bullards, near what is now the world-famous Bandon Dunes golf complex.

On the heels of the miners, homesteaders began moving into the area. One of them, Robert W. Bullard, for whom the bridge is named, migrated to Coos County from Winnesheik County, Iowa, in 1877. He first settled in the little Coquille Valley town of Arago, located about six miles south of

Coquille toward Myrtle Point. In 1882 Bullard established a general store and ferry that operated from the north bank of the Coquille River, where the northern approach to the bridge is now located.[2]

According to historian Nathan Douthit, "The ferry was a small scow that could hold a horse team and buggy. It left from the store and took about 15 minutes to drift downstream with the tide to the opposite bank and to be pulled back again by cable. In later years a gasoline powered winch did the work of pulling the ferry back and forth across the river."

Over time a small settlement grew around the ferry. Bullard's General Store became a U.S. Post Office, and the town of Bullards was born. In the town's heyday the store became the gathering place for local social events. The second floor housed a large hall where weekend dances were held. Entire families from around the area attended these events, the hall bursting with people young and old enjoying music and other entertainment. While adults danced and socialized, the children watched and played. When the children got tired, makeshift beds were provided. "At midnight, a big meal was served, and people went home in the early hours of the morning."[3]

Bullards remained a thriving community center for more than seventy years. It might still be there but for major alterations of Oregon's coastal

125

COQUILLE RIVER BRIDGE
Technical Data

Location: Bandon vicinity, Coos County; Oregon Coast Highway (US 101), Milepost 259.6

Year completed: 1952

Type: Steel through truss with vertical lift

Length: 702 feet

Deck to streambed: 53 feet

Description: Two 30-foot reinforced-concrete deck girders, one 221-foot steel through truss, one 80-foot vertical lift steel deck girder span, one 221-foot steel through truss, four 30-foot reinforced-concrete deck girder spans

Contractor: Carl M. Halverson Inc.

Cost: $626,516

Ownership: State of Oregon

The Coquille River Bridge has a steel through truss with a vertical lift.

highway routes beginning in the 1950s. The original Oregon Coast Highway, completed in 1932, followed the well-established county road that ran inland between Coos Bay and Bandon through the Coos County seat of Coquille. A secondary route, Seven Devils Road, which is still in use, followed an old road known as the Randolph Trail that ran from Coos Bay through Charleston, meandering along the ocean to Bullards and the ferry.

By the early 1950s, traffic volume along this route began to overwhelm the old ferry. In 1952, Coos County and the Oregon State Highway Department agreed to construct a new bridge across the Coquille River at Bullards.[4] Whether by plan or the lack thereof, when the bridge was completed in 1954, the little community of Bullards disappeared. Born of one transportation conveyance—a ferry, the little town died of another—a bridge.

Then, in 1960, after years of planning, a new US 101 segment bypassed Coquille, connecting

Coos Bay and Bandon directly, saving motorists nearly twenty miles of travel. With this change, the Coquille River Bridge became an integral part of the Oregon Coast Highway.

The Bullard Family cemetery lies near the bridge.

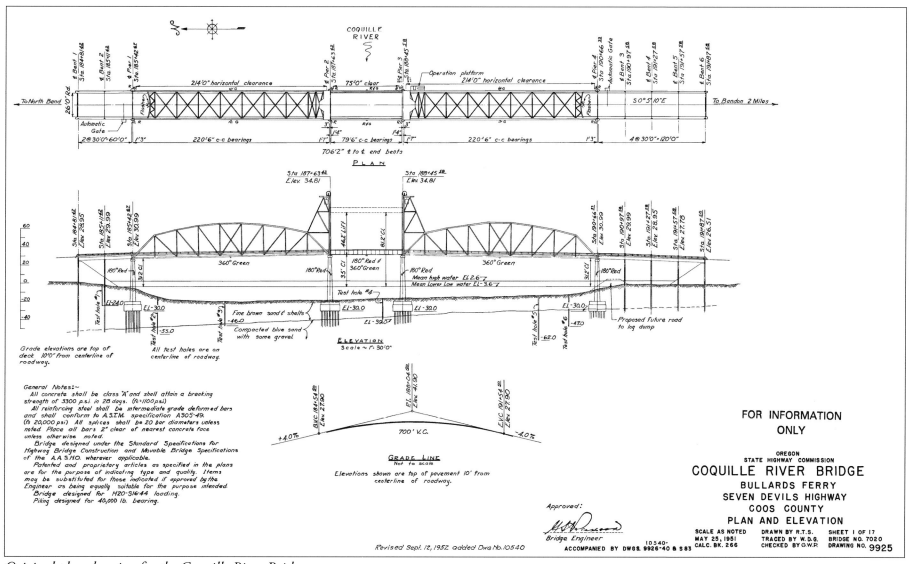

Original plan drawing for the Coquille River Bridge.

The last vestige of the community of Bullards now resides in Bullards State Park, located on the west side of the highway at the north end of the bridge, accessed by Old Ferry Lane. On a lonely hillside at the north end of the park sits a diminutive cemetery bearing the gravestones of three related pioneer families. Robert Bullard is buried here along with his wife, Malinda, a descendant of the Hamblocks and Longs, two of their six children, and other relatives.[5] The cemetery is not easy to find, so ask a park attendant.

The park, worthy of a visit in its own right, provides both day use and overnight camping. It offers a restful area for picnics and walking, as well as some good spots for viewing the bridge. At the park's western edge near the mouth of the river sits the picturesque Coquille River Lighthouse. Constructed in 1896, it was the last of eight lighthouses constructed along the Oregon coast and remained in commission until 1939. After decades of neglect it now has been renovated and is open for visitors, displaying a pictorial history of the area.

The Elk River Bridge demonstrates how a bridge of simple design can blend comfortably within a particular site.

31

Elk River Bridge

A COMMON TOUCH

Sited three miles north of Port Orford, Elk River Bridge demonstrates how a bridge of simple design can blend comfortably within a particular site. This unadorned reinforced-concrete deck girder span crosses a wide, low-lying meadow that cradles the river within it, neither detracting from nor overwhelming the site's tranquil beauty. This stretch of road sports two other bridges of similar design, contemporaries of the 1969 Elk River Bridge; Floras Creek Bridge, ten miles north, dates to 1967, and the Sixes River Bridge, two miles north, to 1971.

Advertised locally as the Gateway to America's Wild River Coast, Elk Creek Bridge sits near the access road to Cape Blanco State Park, Oregon's westernmost headland. Near the Elk River State Fish Hatchery, that breeds species of salmon and trout, the bridge spans one of the favorite local fishing holes. In 2009, the pristine waters of the north and south branches of the Elk River and the nearby Sixes River were designated part of the Copper Salmon Wilderness area.

According to *Oregon Geographic Names*, Elk River derives from Oregon's territorial days, obviously from the many elk seen in these parts. Sightings in the early years of the twenty-first century are no longer so common in this area, but for anyone interested, the best elk viewing for motorists exists at a preserve along the Umpqua River, a few miles upriver from Reedsport and the Umpqua River Bridge.

ELK RIVER BRIDGE

Technical Data

Location: Port Orford vicinity, Curry County; Oregon Coast Highway (US 101), Milepost 297.0

Year completed: 1969

Type: Reinforced-concrete deck girder

Length: 680 feet

Deck to streambed: 34 feet

Description: One 80-foot, four 130-foot, one 80-foot reinforced-concrete deck girders

Ownership: State of Oregon

The Brush Creek Bridge features a graceful three-rib open spandrel arch.

Brush Creek Bridge

RETRO RENAISSANCE

A few miles south of Port Orford in the Humbolt Mountain area, four highway bridges cross various branches of Brush Creek. These simple reinforced-concrete deck girder spans built in the 1950s seemed of little interest or merit. Recently, however, when one of these bridges along US 101 needed replacing, the Bridge Engineering Section Preservation Team of the Oregon Department of Transportation (ODOT), decided that its replacement would be anything but commonplace.

The new Brush Creek Bridge features a graceful three-rib, open-spandrel arch reminiscent of the Conde B. McCullough era, and happily heralds a new direction for coastal bridges. For the first time in decades, even secondary bridges are benefiting from ODOT's renewed interest in bringing quality designs to coastal bridges.

Without copying McCullough, the new Brush Creek Bridge follows some of McCullough's basic bridge design principles. For example, the deck arch is a much more pleasing design than the girder or slab. Second, some ornamentation usually is preferred. While McCullough typically utilized the Art Deco motif fancied by his era, Brush Creek Bridge's ornamentation reflects a more modern, yet retro look, featuring unusual rail stanchions and solid concrete rails with decorative recessed-arch relief panels. And the superficial arched railings are reminiscent of McCullough touches utilized at Rocky Creek and Depoe Bay.

Designed by Robert Kaspari, this span uses stainless steel reinforcement in the deck and beams, and microsilica-modified concrete elsewhere in the bridge to fight off corrosion. Opened in 2000, it is the first bridge in the Oregon highway system designed to last 120 years.

BRUSH CREEK BRIDGE

Technical Data

Location: Humbolt Mountain vicinity, Curry County; Oregon Coast Highway (US 101), Milepost 306.35

Year completed: 2000

Type: Reinforced-concrete deck arch

Length: 218 feet; 129-foot main span

Deck to streambed: 39 feet

Description: One 44-foot prestressed reinforced-concrete slab, one 129-foot reinforced-concrete deck arch, one 44-foot prestressed reinforced-concrete slab arch support, one 56-foot prestressed reinforced-concrete slab, one 17-foot reinforced-concrete slab, one 56-foot prestressed reinforced-concrete slab

Designer: Robert Kaspari

Ownership: State of Oregon

Reinhart Creek Bridge's steel deck truss is the only one of its exact type along the coast.

Reinhart Creek Bridge
HUMBUG TREASURE

Reinhart Creek Bridge spans a deep ravine just south of Humbug Mountain, which until recently (in geologic time) was a coastal island but now presides as the most dominant headland south of Cape Blanco. This desolate, windswept Curry County outback attracts motorists, sightseers, and hikers with its striking views and scenic trails.

Creating an important but often overlooked contribution to all this activity, Reinhart Creek Bridge accommodates all comers. Its steel deck truss looks similar to Thomas Creek Bridge thirty-five miles south, but without the high towers. Although similar to several bridges built by Conde B. McCullough in the 1930s (especially a group along Elk Creek in Douglas County), Reinhart, built in 1954, is the only one of its exact type along the coast.

Reinhart Creek is named for Herman and Charles Reinhart, who homesteaded on the creek about three miles north of Sisters Rocks in 1854.[1] Born in Prussia, the brothers immigrated with their family to New York City in 1840, where their father worked as a baker. In 1848 the family moved to a farm in Lake County, Illinois, but the parents died soon after. In 1851 the brothers headed west looking to strike it rich mining for gold. While their quest for financial wealth wasn't realized, they lived rich lives, which Herman (1832-1889) recounts

in a memoir published as *The Golden Frontier* (University of Texas Press, 1962).

An interesting read about the early days in Oregon and the West, Reinhart describes the many adventures he experienced with his brother as miners, ranchers, bartenders, and storekeepers, who followed the lure of gold from Oregon's Siskiyou Country north to Canada's Fraser River and then back to the frontier mining areas of Idaho and Montana.

In 1866 Herman dissolved his business relationship with his brother in Umatilla County, Oregon, never to see him again. He headed east, traveling through Montana, Illinois, Pennsylvania, and New York. After this peripatetic life, in 1871 he settled down in Chanute, Kansas, where he married, had children, owned a livery stable and restaurant, and served his community as councilman, marshal, street inspector, and fire warden, all of which is included in his remarkable memoir.[2]

REINHART CREEK BRIDGE
Technical Data

Location: Curry County, Humbug Mountain vicinity; Oregon Coast Highway (US 101), Milepost 311.4

Year completed: 1954

Type: Steel deck truss

Length: 356 feet

Deck to streambed: 140 feet

Description: One 56-foot reinforced-concrete deck girder, one 220-foot steel deck truss, two 40-foot reinforced-concrete deck girders

Ownership: State of Oregon

The Euchre Creek Bridge (US 101) is a reinforced-concrete deck girder bridge.

Euchre Creek Bridge (US 101)

CURRY FAVORITE

Euchre Creek Bridge (US 101), a 28-foot wide reinforced-concrete box girder bridge whose central beam sits on ten steel posts, is the only bridge of its type along the coast. Constructed in 2009, the newest bridge along the coast as of this writing, this unusual girder bridge demonstrates how a simple design can sometimes display unusually attractive qualities. It also reflects the special attention Oregon Department of Transportation's Bridge Engineering Section now pays even to smaller bridges, especially along the coast.

According to *Oregon Geographic Names*, the name Euchre comes from the Tututni Indian band *Yukichetunne*, meaning "people at the mouth of the river." While various Anglicized versions of this word were tried over the years, Euchre, the name of a then-popular card game stuck when the local miners began using it.[1]

EUCHRE CREEK BRIDGE (US 101)

Technical Data

Location: Curry County, Humbug Mountain vicinity; Oregon Coast Highway (US 101), Milepost 316.9

Year completed: 2009

Type: Reinforced-concrete deck girder

Length: 90.9 feet

Deck to streambed: 25 feet

Description: One 45-foot prestressed reinforced-concrete slab, one 90-foot prestressed reinforced-concrete box girder, one 45-foot seismic designed prestressed reinforced-concrete slab.

Ownership: State of Oregon

The Euchre Creek Bridge (Ophir Road) is a classic example of an early McCullough reinforced-concrete deck girder bridge.

Euchre Creek Bridge (Ophir Road)

EARLY McCULLOUGH GIRDER

Euchre Creek Bridge (Ophir Road), a classic example of an early McCullough reinforced-concrete stringer (beam) bridge, remains one of few left on the Oregon state highway system.

Sited on Ophir Road (Curry County Road 510), an early Oregon Coast Highway segment, it was bypassed by US 101 but still runs parallel to it for several miles as it crosses Euchre Creek. It's likely that Euchre Creek Bridge has been preserved because of the lighter traffic off US 101.

McCullough softened the profile of the original Euchre Creek Bridge by using "arched girder members with bush-hammered insets, soffit brackets, and precast arched concrete railing."[1] The bridge was built in 1927, the same year he built two of his early classic arched bridges, Depoe Bay and Rocky Creek. Yet in Euchre Creek, the arch motif became strictly ornamental.

Old Euchre Bridge on Ophir Road can be accessed by an exit at the new Euchre Bridge (US 101); the old bridge sits less than a mile off the highway. Once part of the original Oregon Coast Highway, Ophir Road provides another opportunity for motorists to experience what it was like to travel the old coast highway. It meanders through natural terrain, curving, twisting, rising and falling, and passes through what's left of the little community of Pistol River on its way to Brookings.

EUCHRE CREEK BRIDGE (OPHIR ROAD)

Technical Data

Location: Ophir Road, (Curry County Road 510)

Year completed: 1927

Type: Reinforced-concrete deck girder

Length: 90.9 feet

Description: Three 30-foot reinforced-concrete deck girder spans

Designer: Conde B. McCullough

Contractor: D.P. Plymale

Ownership: Curry County

The Rogue River Bridge was the first bridge to cross a major coastal waterway.

Rogue River (Isaac Lee Patterson) Bridge
ROGUE WITH HIGH STANDARDS

Rogue River Bridge, the first of Conde B. McCullough's six major Oregon coast bridge masterpieces, connects the towns of Gold Beach and Wedderburn. It remains today one of the most distinguished, photographed, and beautiful spans in the Northwest. When opened for traffic in 1931, it became the first bridge to cross a major coastal waterway, and the state's largest and most expensive span.[1] The Rogue embodies many features that epitomize the McCullough style: a series of broad, graceful arches constructed of reinforced concrete; smaller arches used as counterpoints; and decorative features such as Art Deco entrance pylons, arch railing supports, and ornate detailing.[2]

By featuring one of the most ancient, appealing, and durable architectural forms—the arch—McCullough's design emphasized tradition, beauty, and stability, qualities intended to boost the confidence of the people who lived in and visited Oregon's coastal communities during the Great Depression of the 1930s.

Of the six Great Depression-era bridges to be built along the coast, the Rogue was the only one completed under President Herbert Hoover's Reconstruction Finance Corporation, created to provide economic assistance to private entities such as banks, railroads, and other key economic institutions to help bolster the nation's depressed economy. President Franklin D. Roosevelt later expanded this concept into the public arena by creating the famous Public Works Administration (PWA), which would soon finance five additional major coastal bridges, commonly known as the Oregon Coast Bridges Project, and bring much needed jobs to the area.

The Rogue set a high design standard for the five bridges that were to follow, and proved to have a significant influence on the development of the Oregon Coast Highway and the opening of Oregon's southern coast. Although it opened for traffic in December 1931, the bridge's formal ceremonies, including its dedication to Oregon Governor Isaac Lee Patterson (1859-1929), needed to be postponed until May 28, 1932, in order to coincide with the opening of the newly completed Oregon Coast Highway. The joint opening ceremonies gave rise to an unprecedented celebration that attracted thousands of motorists and spectators from all over the West.

Looking back on this event, which took place more than three-quarters of a century ago as of this writing, one can only imagine the excitement generated by the completion of the long-anticipated coast highway, coupled with the opening of Oregon's largest bridge in a remote corner of the state. Even today, major bridge openings often draw considerable crowds, but the multitude that gathered for the dual openings grew dramatically, likely becoming the largest gathering to that date in Oregon's history.

Two years into the Great Depression, people everywhere were desperate for any encouraging economic news. For Oregonians, after more than

ROGUE RIVER BRIDGE

Technical Data

Location: Gold Beach–Wedderburn, Curry County; Oregon Coast Highway (US 101), Milepost 327.5

Date completed: 1931

Type: Reinforced-concrete deck arch

Length: 1,898 feet

Deck to streambed: 82 feet

Description: Seven 230-foot open-spandrel, rib-type, reinforced-concrete arch spans, each 47 feet high, flanked by reinforced-concrete arch viaduct approaches, each 144 feet long; a 27-foot roadway; and 3.5-foot raised pedestrian walkways

Bridge engineer: Conde B. McCullough

Assistant Bridge engineer: G.S. Paxson

Resident engineer: Marshall Dresser

Chief designer: O.A. Chase

Contractor: Mercer-Fraser Construction Co., Eureka, California

Cost: $539,615

Ownership: State of Oregon

Renovation contract: Cathodic protection system in 2003

Construction of the bridge.

Historic view of the completed bridge.

Detail of decorative pylon.

Approach pylons leading to main span.

twenty years of planning and construction, the completion of the coast highway generated exciting news in itself. Combined with the opening of the coast's first major bridge, the event became a once-in-a-lifetime celebration and public relations bonanza. For residents of the southern coast, the festivities provided an opportunity to host a major transportation milestone while showcasing the spectacular natural beauty of this largely undiscovered coastal corner of Oregon.

Regional interest grew as plans for the event unfolded. Automobile clubs solicited their members from Oregon, Washington, and California. Local booster organizations promoted the event with press releases published in newspapers throughout the Northwest, and word of mouth took it from there. As the celebration grew near, the number of people committed to attending the festivities rose beyond all expectations, and residents of the tiny towns of Gold Beach and Wedderburn began to feel overwhelmed by the deluge of visitors preparing to flood the area.

Robert Withrow, editor of the local newspaper, the *Curry County Reporter*, held the position of secretary of the bridge and highway Celebration Committee. It became a thankless job. The small, poverty-stricken local towns were suddenly faced with the cost of hosting thousands of people for the dual openings. Feeling impecunious and desperate, they solicited state officials for financial assistance to accommodate the celebrants heading their way, only to be rebuffed. One cannot help but be moved by the frequent, and often despairing, correspondence between Withrow and state public officials from whom he sought financial assistance for the celebration. At one point an exasperated Withrow complained that, "It appears that…I am the 'goat.' It was my understanding…that all matters pertaining to construction of grand stand and barriers would be handled by the state highway department as the state's share in the cost of the 'state

View facing west of the Rogue River Bridge.

celebration.' I understood that your men would make all arrangements for lumber and erect the stand and that the committee would be relieved of this work and any cost attached thereto….

"I am working from 6 AM until 12 midnight on this celebration. I have little assistance locally, for our small bunch of men in Gold Beach are having a hard time of it making a living….

"We are going the limit and as this is a state function, we expected some little assistance. But if the poor old state highway department which built the bridge is not interested enough to provide us with even a grand stand, then God help us all."[3]

Finally, some moral support came from A.W. Norblad, former governor and head of the Oregon Coast Association. He wrote to Leslie M. Scott, chairman of the Oregon Highway Commission, on behalf of the communities, requesting $250 for the event.[4] This was also rejected on the grounds that the commission had no "legal authority to expend funds for purposes of this kind."[5]

Though the details remain cloudy, it appears that the local communities were ultimately provided some financial support and that the festivities were a great success. According to a local newspaper account:

> The greatest throng which ever assembled in Southwestern Oregon
> was here for the historic event. Fully 6,000 were in attendance. They

came from every corner of the Pacific coast to travel over the west's most scenic route and to take part in the dedication of Oregon's greatest highway bridge. Hundreds of cities and towns of Oregon were represented. There were delegations from Washington, and as far north as British Columbia. The Redwood Empire to the south in California was represented by hundreds who came in a great caravan that assembled at Crescent City.[6]

With the 1932 elections looming, even President Herbert Hoover figured into the festivities. Oregon Senator Fredrick Steiwer wrote President Hoover, requesting that he participate in the ceremony.[7] As the event unfolded, various newspapers reported that either Hoover or Vice President William Curtis "pressed the historic gold telegraph key in the White House which sent a flash of electricity across the continent, breaking the barrier of evergreens and signifying to the world that the Rogue River bridge was a complete structure and open for travel."[8]

But the truth is harder to discern. My research with the White House and the Hoover Institute at Stanford University reveals that while both President Hoover and Vice President Curtis were in Washington on May 28, there is no official record that either man took part in the opening ceremony. Interestingly, however, the vice president called on the president at 3:45 PM Eastern Standard Time, but the subject of

Detail view of one of the bridge pylons.

the conference was not announced.[9] That would have been 12:45 PM Pacific Standard Time, only an hour and 15 minutes after the announced bridge opening time set for 11:30 AM PST, or 2:30 PM EST. Was the opening delayed? Steiwer's letter to Hoover mentions a 2:30 PM PST opening, yet a local newspaper article stated 11:30 AM as the arrival time for the motor caravan, at which time the evergreen barrier would be dropped.[10] Whether Hoover, Curtis, both, or neither pressed the golden key

we may never know, but somehow the barrier was dropped and the bridge officially opened.

The monumental new bridge and the newly completed coast highway would soon have a profound impact on the remote southern coastal towns whose residents longed for a more dependable link to the outside world. The Rogue demonstrated the benefits of crossing the major coastal waterways with bridges rather than ferries. For local residents and tourists alike, ferries had become bottlenecks to an increasing flow of traffic. Local residents wanted to attract more tourists; motorists wanted fewer delays. A study prepared by the Oregon State Highway Department in the fall of 1935 showed a 76 percent increase in traffic over the Rogue River Bridge compared to projections for ferry service during the same period.[11] This and other studies helped promote further bridge construction along the Oregon coast. Within four years seven of the eight major waterways along the Oregon coast would be bridged, leaving only the mighty Columbia River between Oregon and Washington without a bridge.

The Rogue also receives acclaim for a unique technical innovation used in its construction. On the bridge's fiftieth anniversary in 1982, the American Society of Civil Engineers designated it a National Historic Civil Engineering Landmark, recognizing for the first time in America, McCullough's use of the Freyssinet technique of prestressing concrete arches.

During the early years of the twentieth century, noted French bridge engineer Eugène Freyssinet perfected a method for stabilizing reinforced-concrete bridge arches. He applied

it to sites in France as early as 1908, where traditional reinforced-concrete structures with relatively flat deck arches like those in the Rogue River Bridge would experience elastic shortening, or downward deflection, in the roadway once their false work was removed. To compensate for this sagging, Freyssinet devised a method of leaving the crowns of the arches open during construction. Using hydraulic jacks, he was able to post-tension, or adjust, the arch ribs after the load of the roadbed was in place. This method was intended not only to strengthen and improve the smoothness of the roadway in traditional arch bridge construction but also to reduce costs, which was important to McCullough. Ultimately, higher labor expenses more than offset savings in material costs, but the bridge did benefit from more slender arch ribs than the traditional arch bridges of the time. Nonetheless, this would be the only bridge in the United States to be constructed using this method.[11]

Although the Rogue was finally dedicated to the memory of Isaac Lee Patterson, who was governor from 1927 to 1929 and died in office, the Coos Bay chapter of the Daughters of the American Revolution petitioned the Oregon State Highway Commission to name the bridge for R.D. Hume, an early settler and entrepreneur in the Gold Beach area, who named Wedderburn for his Scottish ancestral home.[12]

At his request, Hume was buried on the rock outcropping where the Wedderburn approach to the bridge now stands. Although the site is still known as Hume's Rock, his body was removed and buried beside Mrs. Hume after her death.[13]

View facing east of Pistol River Bridge.

144

37
Pistol River Bridge
EARLY GUN CONTROL

At the southern end of what has now become known as Oregon's Gold Coast, generally considered to be the hundred miles between Bandon and Brookings, Pistol River crosses US 101 about ten miles south of Gold Beach. The Pistol River Bridge, a rather attractive deck girder or beam bridge, whose straight lines provide an interesting counterpoint within the rolling, sandy terrain surrounding the bridge, now the Pistol River State Park. At the southwest end of the bridge a large parking area provides access to the river, sandy beaches, and excellent views of the river and bridge.

According to *Oregon Geographic Names*, in a skirmish during the Rogue River Wars a soldier named James Mace lost a pistol in the river and, improbably, that loss named the river. Similar to the town of Bullards, one hundred miles north, a community developed around the mouth of the Pistol River. It status as a town was conferred when a post office was established in 1927, the same year Conde B. McCullough built many of his early bridges along the coast.

PISTOL RIVER BRIDGE
Technical Data

Location: Gold Beach vicinity, Curry County; Oregon Coast Highway (US 101), Milepost 339.1

Year completed: 1962

Type: Reinforced concrete deck girder

Length: 570 feet

Deck to streambed: 34 feet

Description: Two 60-foot reinforced-concrete deck girders, one 80-foot, two 100-foot, one 80-foot reinforced-concrete box girder, and two reinforced-concrete deck girder spans.

Ownership: State of Oregon

The Thomas Creek Bridge is one of only two steel tower bridges on the Oregon Coast Highway.

Thomas Creek Bridge
OREGON'S HIGHEST

Spanning a deep, narrow ravine eight miles north of Brookings, Thomas Creek Bridge holds title as Oregon's highest bridge. At 345 feet above the creek bed, it surpasses by 50 feet its nearest rivals, Conde B. McCullough's famed Crooked River (High) Bridge near Madras, and its new companion, the Crooked River Bridge completed in 2000.

Constructed in 1961, Thomas Creek is one of only two steel tower bridges on the Oregon Coast Highway, and the only one to employ a steel deck truss. (The other, Necarney Creek Bridge near Arch Cape, employs steel deck girders.)

Traveling at highway speed, motorists cross Thomas Creek Bridge in less than ten seconds. Given the narrow, tree-covered ravine and the level, undistinguished superstructure of the bridge, there is little to alert motorists to the bridge's extraordinary height and unusual features.

To fully experience this bridge, visitors must park and walk to its center. Peering down from the bridge's center atop the latticed steel towers that support the bridge, Thomas Creek appears only as a slim, silvery rivulet running between the towers far below. But be forewarned. Walking across this bridge is recommended only for those with a strong constitution, for even with the comforting security of the handrail to grasp, only liars and latent "leapers" can contemplate the dizzying drop without being gripped by acrophobia. Originally, the high-pitched wail of rubber tires crossing the then steel-grilled roadway inspired one reporter to dub it "the screaming bridge."[1]

The bridge's great height required unusual construction techniques and special workers. A newspaper article of the period reports that the bridge was built from the top down, beginning with a bridge section that cantilevered out from the south abutment at highway level, supported by towers of false work that were later removed as the permanent steel towers replaced them. Cranes were positioned at the end of these sections to raise the steel members of the towers as they rose from the creek bed below. To assist in the construction of these towers, laborers had to work off the end of the cantilevered sections, often tottering along a three-foot-wide catwalk with no sides or handrail 350 feet above the creek.[2]

Maintaining the required 25-man crew of ironworkers became a problem. In 1961, ironworkers earned $3.92 an hour, a good wage for the time. The high, dangerous work required workers with almost literally "nerves of steel." Finally Navajo Indians, famed for their experience on other high bridges, such as San Francisco's Golden Gate, came to the rescue to fashion the ironwork. Strangely enough, disputes arose between the Navajo and non-Navajo workers regarding safety nets. The Navajos refused to work with nets, believing that they were bad luck; the non-Navajo workers refused to work without them. As a compromise, the nets were removed for the Navajos until the ironwork was finished and then re-hung for the non-Navajo concrete and carpentry crews.

THOMAS CREEK BRIDGE

Technical Data

Location: Brookings vicinity, Curry County;
Oregon Coast Highway (US 101), Milepost 347.7

Year completed: 1961

Type: Steel deck truss (Warren with verticals)

Length: 956 feet

Deck to streambed: 350 feet

Description: Four 15-foot reinforced-concrete slab spans,
one 265-foot steel deck truss, one 26-foot steel tower,
one 159-foot steel deck truss, one-27-foot steel tower,
one 371-foot steel deck truss, and three 16-foot
reinforced-concrete slab spans; horizontal tubular steel
railings on concrete bases

Designer: Ivan D. Merchant

Contractor: Oregon State Highway Department (now
Oregon Department of Transportation)

Steel fabrication: Bethlehem Steel Corporation, Seattle

Ownership: State of Oregon

Thomas Creek Bridge holds title as Oregon's highest bridge.

Even more vexing were teenage daredevils who snuck onto the bridge after working hours to jump from the roadway into the safety nets. Watchmen were finally hired to keep these hooligans and other curious onlookers off the bridge and out of harm's way.[3]

For local commuters, the bridge's record height likely means less than its record as a commuting time saver. It eliminates one of the coast's most treacherous routes, a tortuous, undulating 37-mile stretch of highway with hundreds of dangerous curves that helped make Brookings, Oregon's southernmost coastal community, seem an isolated and almost inaccessible outpost.

Although renowned as the highest bridge in Oregon, Thomas Creek Bridge represents a fundamental element of bridges: a quicker way across. It may not be one of the more elegant or scenic bridges along the coast, but if you talk to local commuters who save hours in commuting time, Thomas Creek Bridge is the most appreciated bridge on the Oregon Coast Highway.

The Bridge's two steel towers support the steel deck truss.

The Chetco River Bridge is a fully continuous post-tensioned reinforced-concrete box girder bridge.

39

Chetco River (Benjamin A. Martin) Bridge

AWARD WINNER

"Almost a piece of sculpture with qualities far surpassing basic engineering needs," proclaimed the award jury of the Prestressed Concrete Institute when it granted the graceful Chetco River Bridge its Award of Excellence in 1972, one of only seven bridges in North America honored that year.[1] Bearing the name of the local Indian tribe who lived along the lower reaches of the river, the Chetco remains one of the most noteworthy contemporary replacement bridges along the Oregon coast.

Constructed at the beginning of an era when concrete-slab bridge designs from the Siletz (1973) to the Nehalem (1983) were common along the coast, the Chetco easily remains the most distinguished. Although it employs the relatively common reinforced-concrete box girder construction, the Chetco River Bridge demonstrates the benefit that quality design brings to a structure and site. The existing four-lane span became the fourth highway bridge to cross the Chetco River at Brookings, replacing a traditional 46-year-old green, two-lane steel truss bridge built in 1926. Two earlier wooden structures preceded that bridge, the latter of which collapsed in 1925, only ten years after its construction in 1915.[2]

At its opening the bridge was dedicated to B.A. "Dot" Martin, a native son of the Brookings-Harbor area and a long-time employee of the Oregon State Highway Department. Martin began his work for the department in 1925 as a chainman. In the 1930s he rose to be chief locating engineer, whose responsibilities included laying out much of the state's original highway system, including major sections of the coast highway through southern Oregon.[3]

CHETCO RIVER BRIDGE

Technical Data

Location: Brookings south city limits, Curry County; Oregon Coast Highway (US 101), Milepost 357.9

Year completed: 1972

Type: Fully continuous post-tensioned reinforced-concrete box girder

Description: Seven reinforced-concrete box girders with a 240-foot center span flanked by two 190-foot, two 150-foot, and two 97-foot spans; two 3-foot, 4-inch concrete sidewalks

Length: 1,114 feet

Deck to streambed: 88 feet

Construction engineer: J.X. Wilson

Cost: $3,400,000

Ownership: State of Oregon

The Winchuck River Bridge is a reinforced-concrete deck girder bridge.

40

Winchuck River Bridge

BORDERLINE SPAN

Only a half mile from the California border, the Winchuck River Bridge bears the distinction of being the southernmost link in the marvelous and varied chain of bridges that dot the length of the Oregon Coast Highway.

Built in 1965, it is a modest but attractive bridge that typifies a trend common after World War II. Reflecting the general architectural style originally typified by the German Bauhaus School of the 1930s, Winchuck and other similar bridges display the Bauhaus standard of functional simplicity. Hundreds of reinforced-concrete structures similar to the Winchuck were erected throughout Oregon, many of which still remain. These bridges often replaced the steel truss bridges commonly built during the early part of the twentieth century, which in turn replaced many of the open timber and wooden covered bridges of the late nineteenth century.

By 1965, however, this trend had nearly run its course. With technological advances in reinforced-concrete construction, sleek new designs like the Chetco River Bridge—just four miles north of the Winchuck—began to appear. Now, nearly half a century later, bridges like Winchuck River and Euchre Creek, if not yet considered to be structures of historical significance, are at least being recognized as important "period pieces" worthy of preservation.

The name Winchuck is of uncertain origin. McArthur's *Oregon Geographic Names* suggests two possibilities. The name may be derived from the Chinook Indian jargon, wind chuck, or "windy water." According to McArthur, old maps show the name as Wind Chuck. Another interpretation identifies winchuck as the local Native American word for "woman." Take your pick.

WINCHUCK RIVER BRIDGE

Technical Data

Location: Curry County; Oregon Coast Highway (US 101), Milepost 362.6

Year completed: 1965

Type: Reinforced-concrete deck girder

Length: 360 feet

Deck to streambed: 27 feet

Description: One 110-foot, one 140-foot, one 110-foot reinforced-concrete box girder spans with two 3.25-foot sidewalks

Ownership: State of Oregon

The rugged beach and early highway south of Port Orford, 1920.

154

Beaches to Bridges
DEVELOPMENT OF THE OREGON COAST HIGHWAY

In his 1913 Biennial Message to the Oregon State Legislature, Governor Oswald West proposed that, "The ocean beach from the Columbia River on the north to the California state line on the south should be declared a public highway."[1] State Senator Robert S. Farrell carried West's proposal as a bill to the legislature on January 14, 1913, and West signed the bill into law on February 11.

West's intent was to end some misguided earlier legislation allowing the sale of several miles of beaches and to codify what was obvious to transportation policymakers and coastal residents—Oregon's beaches provided a critical link for travel and commerce along the coast. West later promoted the notion that the legislation was intended to preserve the beaches as one of Oregon's most precious natural treasures. He didn't mention this reason in his Biennial Message, but by legislating them a state highway, the beaches remained in the public domain, which accomplished the same thing. As a result, Oswald West became an Oregon legend.[2]

Oswald West, Oregon Governor from 1910 to 1914.

The Ancient Coast Highway

For thousands of years before, Asian immigrants and their descendants, our Native Oregonians, traveled an ancient coastal highway—the beaches and adjacent trails along what we now know as the Oregon coast. Dozens of rivers crossed this north-south corridor, many of whose waters and adjacent land trails became the primary transportation links between the coast and Oregon's inland settlements. Over the centuries these beaches, trails, rivers, and bays combined to create a primitive yet elaborate land- and water-based transportation network through which explorers, trappers, fur traders, and pioneers made their way into western Oregon and along the coast during the late eighteenth and early nineteenth centuries.

Early Historical Accounts of Oregon Beaches as Highways

Ancient accounts of traveling the Oregon Coast Highway survive today only as Native American legend or oral history. The first written accounts of trekking the original beach highway come from early Euro-American explorers and settlers, whose presence began to transform the old highway into a modern one.

Meriwether Lewis and William Clark, commanding their Corps of Discovery, were among the first explorers to find their way overland to Oregon's coast in 1805, following this ancient transportation network of rivers and trails that terminated at the Pacific Ocean. Upon reaching the coast, their party wintered at Fort Clatsop, near what is now Warrenton. During their stay at the fort, Clark penned the first known written account of using the beaches as a "highway."

Describing his quest for a whale that washed up on the beach, Clark wraps a most significant event in Oregon transportation lore with a little Biblical humor. On January 6, 1806, accompanied by Sacajawea, his Shoshone Indian guide, Clark led a small group of men from their winter camp to what is now Cannon Beach in search of the whale, a trek of about twenty miles. Clark's journal describes the group's progress as it moved south along the beach "round Slipery Stones" toward Tillamook Head. Then, Clark noted, "After walking for 2 1/2 miles on the Stones, my guide made a Sudin halt, pointed to the top of the mountain...and made signs that we could not

Beaches were regularly used as primary transportation routes during Oregon's early years.

proceed any further on the rocks but must pass over that mountain."

The party followed an Indian trail up and over Tillamook Head, then returned to the sands of Cannon Beach until it came to a small Indian village near where the whale had perished. Only the skeleton remained, a disappointment to Clark, but he purchased a small portion of the blubber and some oil from the Indians. "Small as this stock is I prise it highly; and thank providence for directing the whale to us; and think him much more kind to us than he was to jonah, having Sent this Monster to be Swallowed by us in sted of Swallowing of us as jonah's did."[3]

Later, John Frost, Alexander McLeod, and the legendary explorer Jedediah Smith all wrote journals of their travels along the Oregon coast.

Smith's journal provides the clearest record of traveling the ancient highway. Using the beach as their primary route, he and his men traveled as the Indians had for thousands of years. When the tides and terrain permitted they preferred the beaches, but insurmountable obstacles, including headlands and rivers, often forced them into using inland connecting trails that served as an integral part of the highway.

Smith's journal begins on May 10, 1828, as he and his 17-man party head in a northwest direction from California along the Trinity River, finally reaching the Pacific Ocean on June 8. They then turn north up the coast, crossing the Winchuck River (probably near the site of the Oregon Coast Highway's most southern bridge) into Oregon on June 23.

Drawing of Jedediah Smith, early Oregon explorer.

A typical example blends the tragic with the mundane:

> MONDAY, June 30th, 1828. We was up and under way in good season, directing our course N.N.W. along the beach 1 mile, then took a steep point of mountain, keeping the same course, and travelled over it and along the beach 6 miles more, and encamped. Lossed on mule last night, that fell in a pitt that was made by Ind[ian]s. for the purpose of catching elk and smothered to death; one other fell down a point of mou[ntain] today and got killed by the fall. The day clear and pleasant.[4]

We know from Smith's diaries that his party, like McLeod's, had many encounters with Indians. Most of these were agreeable, a few were threatening, but then a final, fatal encounter ended the expedition. After covering more than one hundred miles in three weeks, Smith and his men reached the Umpqua River on July 13 and made camp. The next day, Smith and two companions ventured out on a scouting trip, leaving the rest of the party in camp. Indians attacked and killed the remaining men. Smith and his two companions were unharmed and managed to escape and reach Fort Vancouver where, to their surprise, they discovered that another companion had also escaped and reached the fort.

Dr. John McLoughlin, chief factor of the Hudson's Bay Company in Vancouver, sent Alexander McLeod, his lieutenant who had explored the Umpqua River two years earlier, along with Smith, to try to recover the furs and horses taken by the Indians. They were remarkably successful, recovering some 700-800 furs and about 40 horses, along with rifles, traps, clothes and beads. "The most important items recovered, however, were the journals of Jedediah Smith and Harrison Rogers."[5]

Early Roads Along the Coast (1850-1913)

Old Indian routes that Smith and other explorers followed in the 1800s were used and improved by the settlers who followed them. Over time, as communities developed, the old trails became wagon roads, and networks of farm-to-market roads spread around the towns, serving local residents. By the 1850s these towns and the networks of roads radiating from them dotted the length of Oregon's coast. But roads connecting these communities were slow to develop.

Nearly fifty years after Lewis and Clark carved a niche into Oregon's northern coastal frontier, a road developed to the south out of Astoria toward Seaside (the site of Oregon's first beach resort). By 1870, this road developed into a mail route between Astoria and Tillamook, but it narrowed to no more than a trail along Hug Point, Arch Cape, and Neahkahnie Mountain.[6] Roads also linked these northern coastal communities to the population centers of Portland and Vancouver relatively early in the development of the coast highway.

Along the southern coast, some of the hordes that migrated to California during the Gold Rush in the early 1850s spilled into southern Oregon, chasing gold deposits discovered along rivers in the area, most notably near the mouth of the Coquille River. These early residents along the southern coast, especially those around the Chetco and Rogue River areas, were more connected to California's most northern Del Norte County than they were to the territory that would become Oregon's Curry County.

Similarly, the southern coast's population centers of Marshfield, North Bend, and Bandon, all founded around Coos Bay and the Coquille River, were slow to be connected to Oregon's inland valleys by roads. Founded largely by people from San Francisco, they were more closely tied to California than the population centers of Oregon. Not until the opening of the Oregon Coast Highway and the Rogue River Bridge in 1932 did the south coast begin to be fully integrated into Oregon's sphere.

By 1854, a route developed that followed the Umpqua River down to the coast from the area around today's Drain and Elkton to what became Reedsport (now Oregon Highway 38), then heading to Coos Bay, still a popular route today. At its terminus a beach road (now US 101), "…long known simply as the 'Beach Route,' continued to be one of the main arteries of travel into and out of Coos Bay until the coming of the Southern Pacific [Railroad] in 1916."[7] The road connected travelers from the mouth of the Umpqua to Coos Bay along the beach and then on to the mouth of the Coquille River near the little community of Randolph. Early on, this southern section came to be called the Randolph Trail. When the route developed into a wagon road, it somehow became formally designated the "Seven Devils Road (likely a reference to the many curves on the road), which still exists today (see Coquille River Bridge).

South of Bandon "this section has one long beach, from Port Orford to Bandon, but the beach was little used; instead the road followed the sandy terrace a few miles inland where the rivers were much easier to cross and where most of the settlements were located. The 100-foot terrace provided the best site for road, wherever it occurred. The surface is nearly level and usually covered with a veneer of sand."[8] Except for headlands like Humbug Mountain and steep river cuts like Thomas Creek, this plateau created a relatively flat surface that made overland travel south easier and helped preserve the California connection.

Along the central coast, the population center of Newport became the first town to be reached by road when the Corvallis and Yaquina Bay Wagon Road Company formed to build a road from Corvallis to Yaquina Bay in 1864.[9] Most coastal communities, however, existed as remote outposts, since the scant road-building resources were focused primarily on moving people and goods from the interior of the state to and from the coast, not along it.

Road around Hug Point at Cannon Beach.

Along the Coast at the Turn of the Century

By the beginning of the twentieth century, America's love affair with the automobile transformed it from novelty to necessity. Its sudden surge in popularity impacted transportation systems across the country. In Oregon, where horse and buggy roads prevailed, the automotive explosion coincided with Oswald West's term as governor in 1911.

A strong supporter of the national Good Roads movement, West declared that "Oregon will never come into her own in the way of development until she takes steps to improve her highways."[10] In 1913, Governor West created the Oregon State Highway Commission to deal with transportation issues. In the same year he also saw to the formation of the Oregon State Highway Department (now the Oregon Department of Transportation or ODOT), under whose auspices the state began to take responsibility for the hodgepodge of county roads and bridges already existing and for the development of a comprehensive state highway system (see map, page 161).

While the governor's highway commission included a beach highway in the proposed network of major state highways, primary routes such as the Pacific Highway (now Interstate 5) tended to take precedence over less-traveled routes like the Oregon Coast Highway. It would take several years and repeated petitions by coastal transportation advocates before the concept of a continuous coastal highway would receive statewide support. Early efforts to build such a highway along the Oregon coast would prove to be more difficult and time consuming than anticipated.

Stuck in the Mud—the Pathfinder Excursion (1912)

The Pathfinder excursion provides a graphic example of road conditions along the coast in the early 1900s. The first automobile trip from Newport to Siletz Bay developed as a publicity stunt arranged by the Newport Commercial Club to show its support of the Good Roads movement and the deplorable road conditions coastal residents encountered on a regular basis. The round trip covered forty-seven miles of "road" in 22 hours and 40 minutes, barely two miles an hour, and required an extraordinary amount of special gear and ingenuity. According to the two journalists on board, they encountered mundane but troublesome stumbling blocks such

Extricating the 1912 Flanders 20 (Studebaker) during the Pathfinder expedition.

as axle-deep mud, sand, creeks, and logs, not to mention more exhilarating obstacles like impossibly steep grades and dangerously unprotected 100-foot cliffs while crossing over Cape Foulweather.

At one point, to get out of deep sand, the car was run up Fogarty Creek where the sand became like hard dirt, but getting the car out of the creek bed became almost insurmountable. A tramway had to be built from logs, planks, and other beach salvage to get the vehicle out. "The car climbed slowly up and just at the peak fell off and across a huge log, leaving all four wheels in the air. Three times the car was pulled, pried and shoved back on top of the pile of wreckage, only to tip off sideways. Finally, getting desperate, the party rolled a round log close behind the car, a long plank was thrust over this and under the differential. Using the plank as a lever, the rear end of the car was catapulted bodily over the log…." Surprisingly there was little damage to the car.

"While this was being done, 'Sea Lion Charlie,' a well known character of this region, hobbled down from his nearby cabin and gazed in silent wonder at this strange interloper in his isolated domain. As the car, on its fourth attempt crossed the bridge, Charlie exclaimed, 'Well, by—, if I hadn't seen this I wouldn't have believed any living man when he told me.'"[11]

The Coos Bay-Florence Stage Line

In 1916, farther down the coast, another traveler describes a trip taken on the Coos Bay-Florence Stage Line. It begins with a launch crossing from Marshfield to Coos Bay, where passengers then leave the boat and

...embark in a Ford automobile for a spin up the beach and across the sand dunes. Two miles of this part of the journey you don't exactly spin; this 2 miles is over 2-by-12-inch planks laid lengthwise. Where the marsh land makes it necessary, this track is elevated. Ten miles of beach travel brings you to the ford at Tenmile Creek. Here a wagon and two horses are kept to assist the autos across the stream. Unless the water is very low, the front wheels of the machine are run up on a platform attached to the wagon, and in this way water is kept out of the carburetor.

From the ford at Tenmile Creek is another drive of 10 miles to the Umpqua River, which is crossed by steamboat. A six-horse stage is waiting for you on the opposite shore, and this vehicle takes you down the beach another 20 miles. The land journey ends when you embark in a motorboat and cross the Siuslaw to Florence.[12]

Now, that's a trip!

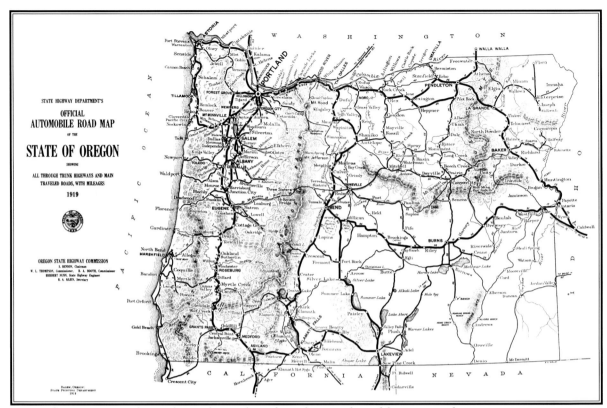

State of Oregon map shows that only north and south coastal road loops existed in 1919.

The Northern and Southern Highway Loops

These firsthand accounts reveal that even after a hundred years of coastal development, there existed no direct highway connection between the north and south coasts. What had developed, however, were northern and southern transportation loops connecting the larger coastal communities with their regional interior population centers. In the north this was Portland; in the south they were Roseburg and Grants Pass.

On August 27, 1916, *The Oregonian* reported the completion of a 300-mile "coast loop" running from Portland southwest through McMinnville and Grand Ronde (now US 99W), then turning north to Hebo and Tillamook. "Leaving Tillamook, the route follows a northerly and westerly direction, through green pastures to Bay City, where the first glimpse of the Pacific is had." Continuing north to Nehalem a spur connected the beach communities of Manzanita and Neahkahnie, but the main highway continued along the north fork of the Nehalem River into Clatsop County, along what is now Oregon 53. Winding through Jewell and Mist, the highway finally connected to the Lower Columbia River Highway back to Portland. [13]

At the southern end of the state, the California connection continued to flourish. A July 23, 1916 article in *The Sunday Oregonian* describes the road conditions of an automobile trip along the southern coast from San Francisco to Coos Bay, the last leg of which made up the longest section of what grew to be Oregon's southern coastal loop. "The road leading on to Gold Beach from Crescent City is pretty fair, although the stages cut up the roads and make them rather rough between Brookings and Gold Beach in wet weather, such as we met coming north. There is good going from Gold Beach to Bandon, and as told in last Sunday's Oregonian, all of the roads in Coos County are in fine shape, as are all except 20 miles of the road leading from Myrtle Point to the connection with the Pacific roadway at Roseburg."[14]

Between these two loops, however, the roads along the coast were patchwork at best, and what roads did exist remained largely impassable in inclement weather. Maps from this period show highway US 101 between Coos Bay and Tillamook as largely unimproved. Along many of these stretches, the beaches were used as the highway and connected with local roads (see map, page 160).

Building the New Oregon Coast Highway 1913-1936

The modern Oregon Coast Highway, from beaches to bridges, evolved over a twenty-three year span beginning with the organization of the Oregon State Highway Department in 1913 and culminating with the construction

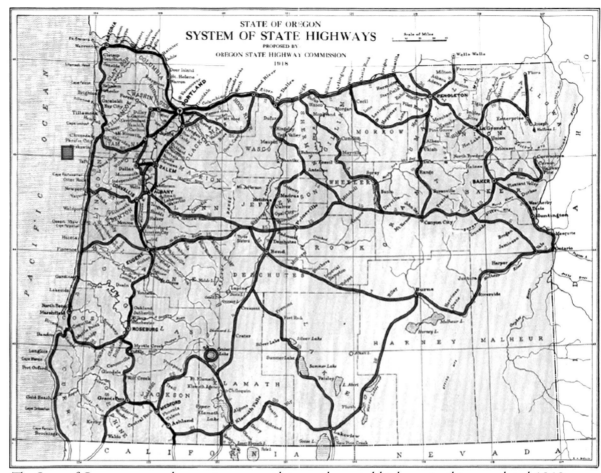

The State of Oregon proposed a continuous north to south coastal highway in this map dated 1918.

of the five major bridges of the Oregon Bridges Project in 1936.

While work on the highway continued slowly and steadily throughout this entire period (much as it continues today), the highway was built in two main stages: First, a passable coast highway, implausibly named the Roosevelt Coast Military Highway, began in 1919 and was mostly completed by 1926. While this largely unimproved highway (only 58 miles were paved) carved out a basic coastal route, it included no bridges over major waterways and offered little

utility as a recreational highway. More than anything, the Roosevelt Highway gave substance to what until then had been simply an inchoate idea. The second stage of the highway began with the tremendous momentum created by the celebrated dual openings of a completed coast highway and the Rogue River Bridge in 1932.

Until the formation of the Oregon State Highway Department, most road construction in the state was the responsibility of the counties. But in 1916, in response to the national demand for better roads to accommodate the public's love affair with the automobile, Congress passed the first Federal Aid Road Act, providing funds to the states for road construction on a matching basis, dollar for dollar. In Oregon, to provide the matching highway funds, bonds were sold, a tax of one cent a gallon was placed on gasoline, automobile license fees were added, and a property tax kicked in $10 million annually. [15]

Men and women take a break during construction in the early 1940s.

Oregon Coast Highway under construction near Rocky Creek Bridge.

The first serious proposal for a coast highway had an unexpected purpose—military protection along the coast. Military roads played a significant role in the development of transportation routes throughout the West, and the idea of a military highway along the coast initially found supporters as early as 1915, as the United States watched the outbreak of hostilities in Europe lead up to World War I. [16]

With the outbreak of war in Europe, a military highway to protect the West Coast from an improbable German attack was sparked by the decoding of the Zimmermann Telegram, a 1917 proposal from Germany to Mexico offering to help reclaim land taken from them by the United States. The idea was ignored by Mexico but angered Americans, strengthening U.S. public support for war against Germany. [17]

The two most southern coastal counties, Coos and Curry, whose historical isolation from mainstream Oregon resulted largely from inadequate roads, threw their support to a military coastal highway. In 1917 Ira Smith, State Senator for the two counties, seized the moment and petitioned the state legislature to construct a coast highway to connect them to Oregon's northern coastal communities and central population centers. Smith's petition declared that, "Whereas the people of the Pacific coast states urgently request the building and maintaining of a military highway along the Pacific coast from the Canadian border to the Mexican border for military necessities and defense such as supplying coast forts with guns and ammunition, the handling of artillery, ammunition and mobilizing troops in the event of an invasion…that provision be made for the building and maintaining of such military roads." [18]

Other supporters included Governor James Withycombe, a supporter of the Good Roads movement and a state highway system. Although a coast highway was not mentioned in his 1915 inaugural address, by 1918 the governor threw his support behind the proposed highway. [19] His support along with many others largely resulted from the United States declaration of war in 1917.

Caterpillar hauling snags on the coast highway in Tillamook County in 1922.

These early coast highway supporters helped to generate interest for the concept, but progress with the highway remained painfully slow. The highway needed an advocate, a person of stature to champion its cause. That person became attorney Ben F. Jones, state representative for Lincoln and Polk Counties and the first president of the Oregon Coast Highway Association. Leslie Scott, then chairman of the Oregon State Highway Commission, memorialized Jones at the joint Rogue River Bridge and Oregon Coast Highway openings in 1932. Jones's persistent efforts regarding transportation issues resulted in getting the Oregon Legislature to pass the $2,500,000 bond to build the Roosevelt Coast Military Highway. His tireless campaign to build a highway along the coast earned him the title "Father of the Roosevelt (Oregon) Coast Highway."[20]

Unfortunately, Jones did not live to see his coastal highway dream completed. He died unexpectedly of a heart attack on March 9, 1925. Rocky Creek Bridge, one of Conde McCullough's most famous smaller arch bridges, was dedicated to him in 1927. His colleague I.S. Smith, however, did live to see the highway fully completed, bridged, and paved. He died in 1950 at the age of 91.[21]

Theodore Roosevelt Coast Military Highway

Through the efforts of I.S. Smith, Ben Jones, and others, a realistic plan for the development of a coastal highway finally began to take shape by 1917. From its inception, however, the Roosevelt Coast Military Highway was riddled with controversy. First, its funding was based on speculation that the federal government would appropriate the matching $2.5 million to build the highway to protect its Pacific shoreline. Second, there were troubles with the name. Exactly how the name evolved is unclear. Theodore Roosevelt's recent death and the suggestion of a military attack along the coast likely influenced highway boosters to promote Roosevelt's "Rough Rider" image and the need for "military" action to attract the necessary funds from what was becoming a more military-minded federal government.

Ultimately, the federal government never came through with the state's request for matching funds. When the war ended and federal funding was not forthcoming, the highway's Roosevelt name and military designation lost their value. Nonetheless, for the next ten years (the name outlasting its funding scheme), the highway continued to be called the Roosevelt Coast Military Highway, often shortened to Roosevelt Coast Highway.

Building the Coast Highway
1919-1932

Although the federal government did not offer to match the $2.5 million dollars requested by the Oregon legislature to build the Roosevelt Coast Military Highway, other federal, state, and county funding materialized, and the highway began its long journey toward completion.

By 1924, there were only 60 miles of paved road along the Roosevelt Highway and 136 miles of graded road surfaced with rock and gravel. Nearly half of the 400 total miles along the coast still needed to be improved. Official highway department reports at the time declare that, "Over unimproved portions between Hauser in Coos County and Taft in Lincoln County, existing roads paralleling the coastline are available only in disconnected sections and through travel is possible only when use is made of the ocean beaches over a considerable part of the distance."[22]

Bridges, of course, also played a significant role in the evolving Oregon Coast Highway. Until the creation of the Oregon State Highway Department in 1913, most bridges in Oregon were built by counties. One bridge from this era, West Beaver Creek Bridge, constructed in 1914, still exists on the coast highway (see West Beaver Creek Bridge). At the north end of the highway, just outside Astoria, two of Conde B. McCullough's early and still surviving bridges, Youngs Bay Bridge, constructed in 1921, and its neighbor the Lewis and Clark River Bridge, constructed in 1924, replaced earlier wooden county bridges. But many early bridges along the coast were haphazard and

Original wooden bridge on Neahkahnie Mountain.

poorly engineered, such as this early bridge on Neahkahnie Mountain (see photo above). Later, and farther down the coast, the Depoe Bay and Rocky Creek bridges were constructed in 1927, and Cape Creek Bridge, a part of the "Million Dollar Mile" that crossed Heceta Head, was completed in 1931. These bridges became critical links in the development of a continuous coast highway.

Driving the Coast in a Day

In 1929, seventeen years after the Pathfinder trip, another group set out to drive the length of the Oregon coast in one day. The stated purpose of the trip was to "prove that the ten-year-old Roosevelt Coast Military Highway had been greatly improved just since 1926, but needed far more work before it was really 'navigable.'" In truth, they were out to best a similar earlier trip made in 1926, when Arthur D. Sullivan, automobile editor for *The Oregonian,* and an associate drove from Astoria to Crescent City, California, a trip that took four days and a total of 57 hours of driving time. That trip had been hit with heavy rains, which turned un-surfaced sections of the road into a "sea of sticky gumbo."

They also confronted "exasperating delays by construction work, long detours over mountain roads and along ocean beaches, being pulled out of mud holes by teams of horses, and putting up at small-town hotels."

Participants in the 1929 trip included Ray Conway, public relations director for the Oregon State Motor Association; Charles E. Nims, Oregon representative for the Portland Cement Association; John Weiser, public relations representative for Marquette Automobiles; and Lawrence Barber, the new automobile editor of *The Oregonian*. Two automobiles were enlisted, a 1929 Marquette touring car provided by the Buick-Marquette dealer in Portland, and a Buick sedan owned by Nims, who was interested in selling cement for road building.[23]

Whereas the 1926 trip from Astoria to Newport took a full day, the 1929 team, enjoying dry weather and improved asphalt roads, made it in just over four hours. At 8:00 AM, five hours after leaving Astoria, the team "drove the two cars onto the Yaquina Bay Ferry, the first of six ferries we had to ride that day. We pulled off at South Beach onto a corduroy road, which consisted of planks or logs laid transversely over soft, sandy ground. We followed a new grade for four miles, then detoured on a hard-packed beach to Seal Rocks. Back inland, we drove on corduroy again for a mile or more, then returned to the beach."

The team sped on to Waldport, Yachats, and Florence, averaging about ten miles per hour. From Yachats to Florence the road "wound around the ocean face of Cape Perpetua and

Heceta Head, the last real wilderness on the coastal route. At times the trail was laid close to the beach; 10 minutes later it might be 500 feet up on a ledge of the bluffs high above the pounding surf."

They took their third ferry across the Siuslaw River at Florence and then motored on down to Reedsport. "The ferryman, A.F. Smith, collected 50 cents a car and assured us that nobody before us had attempted to drive from

South of Port Orford, Curry County in 1920.

Astoria to Crescent City in one day, as far as he knew."

The team logged 244 miles in 13.5 hours, compared to 29 hours by the 1926 group. But it was still another 173 miles to the California border. The 1926 group experienced all sorts of problems between Florence and Coos Bay, "including loading of their car on a barge and hiring a tug to tow them to a sandspit at the mouth of the Umpqua River—where the car mired down in soft sand upon being unloaded. They hired a team of horses to pull the car out. They ran down the beach several miles, bogged down again and once more had to hire horses to pull them out. They finally arrived at the Coos Bay Ferry landing 17 hours after leaving Reedsport." The 1929 team made the same trip in one hour and five minutes over a newly completed macadam road, a fitting testimonial for good roads.

They completed the rest of the trip without delay and rolled through Gold Beach at 10:00 PM, after waiting an hour in Wedderburn for the ferry. "We had a winding dirt mountain road between Pistol River and Brookings. The Marquette rolled up to the Lauff Hotel at 12:10 AM, 21 hours and 15 minutes after leaving Astoria Hotel...we figured our net driving time was a little over 18 hours and we were proud."[24]

They had reason to be proud, for even with the improvements made on the route since 1926, the idea that one could travel the length of the Oregon coast by car in one day must have stretched the motoring public's credulity. It was, however, a very long day.

A Completed Oregon Coast Highway

By 1930 the general condition of the coast highway was paved from Astoria to Seaside, improved to Newport, unimproved and mostly very poor from Newport to Coos Bay, and then improved again to the California line. There was still only a track from Coos Bay to Newport, but this was on sandy surfaces, making it possible to travel above the beach in the rainy season, but with the risk of becoming stuck in the sand.[25]

Nonetheless, work on the highway continued to progress, and two years later, on May 28, 1932, a continuous highway running the length of the coast was completed. Speaking at the simultaneous opening of the new coast highway and the dedication of the Rogue River Bridge, Leslie M. Scott, chairman of the Oregon State Highway Commission, declared that "today we have a finished highway...."[26]

The 1932 route, however, remained a far cry from the highway we travel today. Two-thirds of the distance still needed paving. It wandered along natural terrain as a narrow, inadequately graded road in many areas, and still ran many miles inland to avoid headlands such as Neahkahnie Mountain, Cape Perpetua, and Humbug Mountain. Only McCullough's Rogue River Bridge crossed one of the major coastal waterways; the others still depended on the inefficient ferries. But at least there existed a continuous navigable roadway, a legitimate Oregon Coast Highway.

Over time, many unpaved sections of the highway became paved, most without ceremony, but not unnoticed either. Local and statewide periodicals

One may still drive the Rocky Creek Bridge on a bypassed section of the original Oregon Coast Highway.

of the time and the Oregon State Highway Commission Biennial Reports chronicled the continuing work on the highway. For example: "Continued progress has been made on the Roosevelt Coast Highway. South of Newport, the Yaquina Bay-Alsea Bay Unit has been graded and the surfacing placed under contract as cooperative forest highway projects. New ferry slips have been built at both Yaquina and Alsea Bays. Between Waldport and Yachats and south to the Lane County line, the grading has been completed and the surfacing placed under contract. By the end of November, 1930, it is expected that travel may use the entire road south from Newport to the Lane County line, a distance of 26 miles. This will eliminate many miles of beach travel and avoid the danger at the crossings of Beaver Creek, Big Creek and the old elevated tramway on the north side of Alsea Bay."[27]

Conquering the coast by road would have been an enormous achievement for the citizens of Oregon at any time. But completing it in the depths of the Great Depression, along with the Rogue River Bridge, gave Oregonians, as well as people from all over the Northwest, the occasion for an unprecedented celebration (see Rogue River Bridge).

The Oregon Coast Bridges Project

Festivities for the newly opened Oregon Coast Highway and Rogue River Bridge were a great success, but state highway planners had little time to celebrate. The new bridge and highway immediately increased traffic which highlighted the last major impediment to timely travel along the coast—replacing the ferries with bridges at the five remaining major coastal waterways. For the state to attract the tourism it desired, bridges became imperative.

Luckily for the state, a fortunate combination of political and engineering talent soon coalesced to solve this problem. Under a dynamic new president, Franklin D. Roosevelt, federal funds became available through the Public Works Administration (PWA) for public infrastructure projects like bridges. U.S. Senator Charles McNary, R-Ore., and Senate minority leader, led a bipartisan campaign supporting FDR's New Deal programs. With roads a national priority for these funds, McNary encouraged the Oregon State Highway Commission to apply for PWA funds to build five major bridges along the coast.[28]

Oregon also had a friend in Thomas H. MacDonald, chief of the U.S. Bureau of Roads, whose job it was to review such funding requests. Earlier, he had been the head of Iowa's State Highway Commission and, in that capacity, hired a talented young bridge engineer and fellow Iowa State College engineering graduate by the name of Conde B. McCullough. McCullough had since moved to Oregon and by 1932 was working as bridge engineer and assistant state highway engineer for the Oregon State Highway Department.[29]

Flagger in the 1940s. Women were recruited for road construction work during World War II.

167

Historic view of the Rogue River Bridge, 1932.

Oregon's proposal, ultimately known as the Oregon Coast Bridges Project, ambitiously requested funds for the simultaneous construction of five bridges to cross Yaquina Bay, Siuslaw River, Alsea Bay, Umpqua River, and Coos Bay. Responsibility for the design and construction of these bridges, the state's largest construction project, fell to McCullough, who certainly rose to the challenge. Built between 1934 and 1936, these five extraordinary bridges, often referred to as "jeweled clasps in a wonderful string of matched pearls," would become the crowning achievement of McCullough's career.

The Roosevelt Coast Military Highway, never an appropriate name, finally earned its rightful name in 1932 when Lewis A. McArthur, publisher of *Oregon Geographic Names*, presented a bill to the Oregon State Legislature, finally designating the coast route the Oregon Coast Highway. But the modern highway we use today really came into being when the five major McCullough bridges were completed in 1936. From beaches to bridges, the Oregon Coast Highway took nearly a quarter century to build. As it developed into one of the state's principal transportation routes, its multiple benefits changed the texture of the state. The new highway linked coastal communities, creating a coastal identity that didn't exist before; its stunning scenic appeal turned the coast into the state's primary magnet for tourists, generating millions of dollars annually; while the ancient beach highway's designation as a state highway continued to keep its nearly entire length open to the public. In 1991 the Oregon Coast Highway earned acknowledgement as one of the most scenic highways in the country when it was designated a National Scenic Byway.

Today, the highway continues to evolve as a dynamic and ever-changing entity that challenges our politicians, planners, and policymakers who develop Oregon's transportation objectives and garner the necessary funds to reach them; the engineers, contractors, and maintenance crews responsible for the design, construction, and maintenance of our highways and bridges; and the environmental, public policy, and public relations personnel who keep us informed about our state transportation system. But, as we discovered with the loss and replacement of the Alsea Bay Bridge, in the long run, we Oregonians are the most important players, who ultimately determine the future of Oregon's most valued highway treasures—our bridges.

APPENDICES

APPENDIX A

Conde B. McCullough (1887-1946)

Conde Balcom McCullough, Oregon's master bridge builder, served as bridge engineer for the Oregon State Highway Department from 1919 to 1937, and as assistant state highway engineer from 1937 until his death in 1946. During this tenure he was responsible for the design of hundreds of Oregon bridges, many of them now Oregon landmarks.

McCullough was born to Scots-Irish parents John Black McCullough and Lenna Leota (née Balcom) McCullough, on May 30, 1887, in Redfield, Dakota Territory (now South Dakota). His father, a physician and Presbyterian minister, practiced medicine and later studied to become a missionary. His mother reportedly named her first and only child after a French character from a novel she was reading while pregnant, adding her maiden name as his middle name. Early on, his parents moved to Ford Dodge, Iowa, where he received his early education.

A few years after an accident that injured his spine, McCullough's father died unexpectedly when Conde was only 14 years of age, leaving him to assist with supporting the family. After graduating from high school he took a job with the Central Railroad Company as a surveyor's assistant, where he worked for several years before and after graduating from Iowa State College with a civil engineering degree in1910. Working summers with the railroad company provided McCullough his first experience in bridge design.

While in college he was fortunate to study under Anson Marston, who coincidently had also worked for the Central Railroad Company before becoming one of the leading engineering scholars in the country. He believed that engineers should be trained in the arts and languages along with a diverse engineering curriculum, and that classroom studies needed to be augmented with hands-on work experience.

After a brief association with the Marsh Engineering and Construction Company in Des Moines, McCullough worked for the Iowa State Highway Department from 1911 to 1916, first as a design engineer and later as assistant state highway engineer.

It was during this time that McCullough met and worked under Thomas H. MacDonald, the Iowa state highway engineer. During his four-year stint with the highway department, McCullough impressed his boss, and MacDonald advanced him to assistant highway engineer. This became an important connection for McCullough and later for the state of Oregon.

McCullough moved to Oregon in 1916 to join the Department of Civil Engineering at Oregon Agricultural College (now Oregon State University) in Corvallis. By 1918 he had achieved the positions of professor and head of the Civil Engineering Department.

In 1919 McCullough exchanged his university career for one of more practical application as state bridge engineer with the Oregon State Highway Department, a move prompted by a six million dollar bond issue that the Oregon Legislature passed for new highway construction. McCullough knew that highways required bridges. In Oregon, with all its rivers and waterways, especially along the coast, that meant a lot of bridges, and McCullough was eager and able to build them.

McCullough oversaw the design and construction of literally thousands of Oregon's bridges.

First, however, he had to assemble his team. Several Iowa classmates constituted his core group, including Bill Reeves, Orrin Chase, Merle Rosecrans, and E.S. Thayer (in 1931, he and Thayer co-authored a textbook entitled *Elastic Arch Bridges*).

McCullough rounded out his bridge section staff by negotiating an innovative work-study agreement with the Engineering Department at Oregon State. McCullough was allowed to hire several of his senior students in structural engineering two months before graduation. Combining work with study, the students graduated with their class in June.

Once the team was assembled, "Mac" gave them plenty of work to do. In 1922, after three years with the department, McCullough reported that he had designed and supervised the construction of over nine hundred bridges with a total cost of more than seven million dollars.

During these early years with the department, he designed several distinguished bridges, including the Old Youngs Bay Bridge (1921) and the Lewis and Clark River Bridge (1924), two of the oldest and most interesting of the coast bridges, and the Willamette River Bridge at Oregon City (1922). During this period McCullough also designed one of Oregon's most famous bridges, the Crooked River (High) Bridge near Redmond (1926). At 295 feet above the creek bed, this was then the highest bridge in Oregon (at 345 feet, the Thomas Creek Bridge profiled in this book is now the highest).

In 1932 McCullough assumed the added responsibility of assistant state highway engineer while maintaining his position as state bridge engineer. This was a time of extraordinary productivity for McCullough, culminating in the design and construction of six major bridges along the Oregon coast. The first of these was the Rogue River Bridge, the first major bridge on the Oregon Coast Highway. Completed and open at the end of 1931, its formal dedication and opening ceremonies were postponed until May 1932, when a joint opening ceremony was held that attracted thousands of spectators from around the Northwest.

McCullough's old friend and mentor, Thomas H. MacDonald, then chief of the federal Bureau of Public Roads, would be instrumental in funding the Rogue River Bridge under President Herbert Hoover's Reconstruction Finance Corporation, a quasi-public organization designed to provide financial assistance to public works projects in order to help lift the country out of the Great Depression. Under President Franklin D. Roosevelt, this program was reorganized and greatly expanded into the Public Works Administration (PWA). Under the PWA, five additional major coastal bridges, Yaquina Bay, Umpqua River, Alsea Bay, Siuslaw River, and Coos Bay, commonly known as the Oregon Coast Bridges Project, were funded and opened by 1936. Along with these major spans, McCullough also assumed responsibility for the design and construction of dozens of secondary bridges during this period.

A man of considerable intellect and interests, McCullough earned a law degree at Willamette University in 1928 and passed the Oregon State Bar the same year. He also received an

Conde B. McCullough standing on his namesake, the McCullough Memorial Bridge.

honorary doctorate degree in engineering from Oregon State College in 1934.

In 1935 MacDonald once again sought his protégé's talent for bridge construction, this time on foreign shores. McCullough took a leave of absence from the Oregon State Highway Department to sign on with the Bureau of Public Roads in Central America, supervising the design and construction of bridges on the Inter-American (Pan American) Highway.

During his stint in Central America, McCullough constructed three suspension bridges from designs that may have been developed during the planning of the Coos

Bay Bridge. Although the cantilever design finally prevailed at Coos Bay, McCullough did consider suspension designs, the only major bridge type that eluded his legacy in Oregon.

Returning to Oregon in 1937, McCullough continued to serve the highway department as assistant state highway engineer, Glenn Paxson having served as acting state bridge engineer in McCullough's absence. Turning his energies more to research and writing, McCullough authored numerous technical articles and several books, including a two-volume text coauthored with his son John entitled *The Engineer at Law: A Resume of Modern Engineering Jurisprudence* (1946).

McCullough (third from left) poses with unknown associates in bridge portal.

Although bridge design and engineering were McCullough's consuming passion, he was also involved in community activities. He was a Rotarian and Mason, a member of the Salem Chamber of Commerce, and a vestryman at St. Paul's Episcopal Church. In 1945 he was elected chairman of the city's first Planning Commission and a major contributor to a planning document evaluating the impact of growth on Salem.

Stricken with a heart attack in 1942, McCullough was ordered by his doctor to stop smoking and to cut back on his workload. He did so for a while, but soon fell back into his old habits. On May 7, 1946, he had a massive stroke and died, less than a month short of his fifty-ninth birthday.

Bridge building had been McCullough's life, and for a quarter century he oversaw the design and construction of literally thousands of Oregon's bridges. Capped by the Oregon Coast Bridges Project, and with Oregon's great bridge-building boom behind him, it is clear that McCullough knew the lasting imprint he had made on his adopted state.

For his lasting legacy of superior engineering skills and accomplishments, he was honored posthumously in 1947 when the Coos Bay Bridge was rededicated as the Conde B. McCullough Memorial Bridge, a tribute rarely paid an engineer.

For further information on Conde B. McCullough, readers are directed to the resources listed in the Notes for Appendix A on page 192.

APPENDIX B
Cathodic Protection

A technique called cathodic protection protects the reinforcing steel in concrete structures from being infected by salt in the water and air around them. The system works by delivering low electrical currents through zinc coatings applied to the bridges. The currents supply electrons to the iron in the steel and retard its tendency to convert to iron oxide (rust) when the steel comes in contact with saltwater and air from the ocean. This unchecked corrosive process caused the demise of the original Alsea Bay Bridge.

A preventative measure, cathodic protection cannot repair what is already damaged. Employed as a last chance technique to save the old Alsea Bay Bridge, it proved to be too little, too late to save it. Hopefully, this technique (and perhaps other new technological developments), along with vigilant maintenance, will preserve the other coastal bridges for decades to come.

Since 1988, ODOT has installed impressed current thermal-sprayed zinc anode cathodic protection systems on nine bridges: Depoe Bay, Rocky Creek, Yaquina Bay, Cummins Creek, Tenmile Creek, Big Creek, Cape Perpetua, Cape Creek, and Rogue River,

Current cathodic techniques cause a change in appearance of the treated concrete bridges, from their from original color tones to a grey tint, a disturbing alteration in the eyes of some bridge sentimentalists but a small

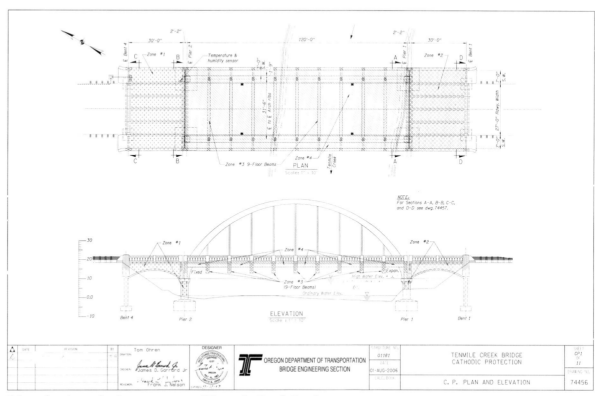

Plans for the cathodic protection of Tenmile Creek Bridge.

A draped Cape Creek Bridge receives a cathodic coating during its restoration in 1989.

price to pay for their preservation. According to James Norman, Oregon Department of Transportation's manager of Environmental Planning, advancements in cathodic coatings may soon be able to match more closely the original bridge color. This new technique is scheduled to be used when the Cape Creek Bridge is to be recoated within the next few years of this writing.

For more information on cathodic protection see Sophie J. Bullard, Stephen Cramer, Bernard Covino, *Final Report: Effectiveness of Cathodic Protection*, Albany, OR, National Energy Technology Laboratory, 2009, ***http://www. oregon.gov/ODOT/TD/TP_RES/docs/ Reports/2009/Efft_Cathodic_Protect.pdf***. Also see Robert W. Hadlow's *Elegant Arches, Soaring Span*, (Corvallis, OR, OSU Press, 2001), 132-133.

APPENDIX C

Bridge Construction Techniques

R.H. Baldock, "Cantilever is Feature of Coos." *Western Construction News* (July 1936). "Bridge Builders' Secrets." *The Oregon Motorist* (May 1936).

Robert W. Hadlow. *Elegant Arches, Soaring Spans.* Oregon State University Press, 2001.

O.A. Chase, "Design of Coast Highway Bridges." *Civil Engineering* 6, no. 10 (October 1936).

C.B. McCullough, "How Oregon Builds Highway Bridges." *The Oregon Motorist* (February 1936).

Conde B. McCullough, "Design of a Concrete Bowstring-Arch Bridge, Including Analysis of Theory, *Engineering News-Record,* August 27, 1931, 337-39.

G.S., Paxson, "Construction of Coast Highway Bridges," *Civil Engineering 6, no.*10 (October 1936).

An interesting website: ***http://www.pbs.org/wgbh/buildingbig/bridge/webography.html***

Glossary of Bridge Terms

ABUTMENT – A substructure element supporting each end of a single span or the extreme ends of a multi-span superstructure and, in general, retaining or supporting the approach embankment.

APPROACH SPAN – The span or spans connecting the abutment with the main span or spans.

ARCH – A curved structure designed to support weight above or below it. Arched bridges may have roadways that cross the top of the arch (deck arches) or move through the arch or at the bottom of the arch (through arches).

BALUSTRADE – A railing or parapet consisting of a handrail on balusters (vertical support members).

BASCULE – A movable bridge in which the roadway deck is counterbalanced by a weight and swings upward like the hinged cover of a box. A bascule bridge may be single-leaf (one-hinge) or double-leaf (two-hinges).

Old Youngs Bay Bridge is a bascule bridge.

BEAM – A linear structural member designed to span from one support to another. One of the major bridge types, along with arch and suspension.

BENT – A substructure unit supporting each end of a bridge span; also called a pier; made up of two or more columns or column-like members connected at their top most ends by a cap, strut, or other member holding them in their correct positions.

BOX GIRDER – A support beam that is a hollow box; its cross-section is a rectangle or square.

BRACKET – An overhanging member that projects from the structure, designed to support a vertical load, usually a sidewalk, or sometimes only the railing.

BUSH-HAMMERED – A treatment to concrete surfaces with a steel-plated instrument which results in a textured surface instead of a flat, smooth surface. This technique is also referred to as pebble-dash.

BUTTRESS – An abutting pier which strengthens a wall, sometimes taking the thrust of an inner pier.

CAISSON (or COFFERDAM) – "Caisson" is the French word for "box." A caisson is a huge watertight box or cylinder, used for construction work under water, made of steel and waterproof concrete, with an open central core. At the base of it is a "cutting edge" of plate steel, which sinks as material is

removed from the waterbed. When filled with concrete, the caisson becomes the foundation, or pier, that supports the bridge's towers.

CANTILEVER – Any rigid structural member projecting from a vertical support, especially one in which the projection is great with relation to the depth, so that the upper part is in tension and the lower part in compression.

CAST-IN-PLACE – Concrete poured within form work on site to create a structural element in its final position.

CATHODIC PROTECTION – See p. 175.

CATWALKS – Temporary foot bridges, used by bridge workers to spin the main cables (several feet above each catwalk), and to attach the suspender cables that connect the main cables to the deck.

CHORD – A horizontal member of a truss.

COLUMN – A vertical structural member that transfers dead and live load from the bridge deck and girders to the footings or shafts.

COLUMN CROSS BRACE – Transverse brace between two main longitudinal members.

CONTINUOUS STRUCTURE – A generally long bridge in which the structure is supported by more than two piers, but still distributes stress over the entire structure.

CORDUROY ROAD – A road constructed of logs laid side by side transversely across the driving surface.

CULVERT – A drain or channel crossing under a road. Generally, culverts are small and constructed of steel or concrete. When they become large and are not continuous under the waterway, they become slab span bridges.

CURTAIN WALL – The outer members in a bridge or approach span, particularly when the configuration differs from the inner members; also called fascia.

DAMPING – The action of reducing the vibration of an object. This tends to return the vibrating object to its original position.

DEAD LOAD – A static load due to the weight of the structure itself.

DECK – The roadway portion of a bridge that directly supports vehicular and pedestrian traffic.

DECK BRIDGE – A bridge in which the supporting members are all beneath the roadway.

DECK TRUSS – A bridge whose roadway is supported from beneath by a truss.

DENTILS – A series of small projecting rectangular blocks, especially under a cornice or other overhanging structure, used for ornamentation.

DIAGONAL – A sloping structural member of a truss or bracing system.

EXPANSION JOINT – A joint designed to provide means for expansion and contraction movements produced by temperature changes, load, or other forces.

FASCIA – See CURTAIN WALL.

FATIGUE – Cause of structural deficiencies, usually due to repetitive loading over time.

FOOTING – The enlarged, lower portion of a substructure that distributes the structure load either to the earth or to supporting piles; the most common footing is the concrete slab; "footer" is a colloquial term for footing.

GIRDER – A main support member for the structure that usually receives loads from floor beams and stringers; also, any large beam, especially if built up.

HALF VIADUCT – A half viaduct is a type of viaduct built into a hillside, where only part of the road is supported by the structure.

Perpetua Bridge is a half viaduct structure.

HANGER – A tension member serving to suspend an attached member.

HINGE – A point in a structure at which a member is free to rotate.

JOINT – In stone masonry, the space between individual stone; in concrete, a division in continuity of the concrete; in a truss, the point at which members of a truss frame are joined.

LATTICE – A vintage railing type that consists of a system of crosshatched diagonals with no verticals.

LIVE LOAD – Vehicular traffic, wind, water, and/or earthquakes.

LOWER CHORD – The bottom horizontal member of a truss.

MAIN BEAM – A beam supporting the spans and bearing directly onto a column or wall.

MEMBER – An individual angle, beam, plate, or built piece intended to become an integral part of an assembled frame or structure.

MOVABLE BRIDGE – A bridge type which opens to allow additional vertical clearance for water navigation.

OSCILLATION – A periodic movement back and forth between two extreme limits. An example is the string of a guitar that has been plucked. Its vibration back and forth is one oscillation.

OVERCROSSING OR OVERPASS – A bridge structure where the principal or subject transportation facility is the upper roadway (of two roadway levels).

PARAPET – A low retaining wall or railing.

PIER – A vertical support or substructure unit that supports the spans of a multi-span superstructure at an intermediate location between its abutments.

PILE – A vertical shaft driven into the ground that carries loads through weak layers of soil to those capable of supporting such loads.

PILE BENT – A row of driven or placed piles with a pile cap to hold them in their correct positions; see BENT.

PLATE GIRDER – A large, solid web plate with flange plates attached to the web plate by flange angles or fillet welds. Typically fabricated from steel.

PONY TRUSS – A low through truss that has no overhead or enclosing truss work. (This word "pony" indicates a scale of measurement, something smaller than standard.)

PORTAL – The clear, unobstructed space of a bridge forming the entrance to the structure.

Portal to Big Creek Bridge.

PRE-CAST GIRDER – Fabricated off site using concrete, reinforcing bar, and post-tensioning cables. These girders are shipped to the construction site by truck and hoisted into place by cranes.

REINFORCED CONCRETE – Concrete with steel reinforcing bars bonded within it to supply increased tensile strength and durability.

RESONANCE – The regular vibration of an object as it responds in step (at the same frequency) with an external force.

RIGID – A rigid connection of metal bridge members that is assembled with rivets. Riveted connections increase the strength of the structure.

SHAFT – A vertical load bearing structure that uses end bearing and friction to support loads.

SKEWED – Slanted or not forming a straight line.

SLAB – A bridge type, generally used in short structures, in which the roadway deck and its support are integral.

SOFFIT – The underside of an overhanging structure.

SPAN – The distance between piers, towers, or abutments. A term often substituted for "bridge."

SPANDREL – The area between the exterior curves of an arch and the roadway.

Spandrel area on the Rogue River Bridge.

STABLE – The ability of a structure to resist forces that can cause material deformation or structural collapse.

STEEL – A very hard and strong alloy of iron and carbon.

STAY – Diagonal brace installed to minimize structural movement.

STRINGER – A longitudinal beam supporting the bridge deck.

Stringers supporting deck of Wilson River Bridge.

STRUCTURE – In the context of this book, a term frequently substituted for "bridge."

SUBSTRUCTURE – The parts of a bridge that are below the bottom of the girders. Pilings, shafts, spread footings, and columns may be part of the substructure.

SUPERSTRUCTURE – The parts of a bridge that are above the bottom of the girders. Girders, bridge deck, and bridge railing are parts of the superstructure.

SUSPENSION – A bridge which suspends the roadway from high towers through a combination of cables. One of the three major bridge types, along with beam and arch.

SWING – A movable bridge which pivots about a vertical axis to allow unrestricted vertical clearance of the navigation channel.

TENSION – A force that pulls or stretches.

THROUGH – Form of bridge in which traffic actually moves through the framework of the bridge.

TIED-ARCH BRIDGE – A truss bridge in which the outward-directed horizontal forces of the arch, or top chord, are borne as tension by the bottom chord, usually the deck itself. In a tied-arch or bowstring bridge, these outward movements are restrained not by the abutments but by the bottom chord, or deck, which ties the arch tips together, rather like the string of an archery bow connects the two tips of the bow. This technique allows arch bridges to be constructed where there are no suitable abutments for a traditional arch. In addition, tied-arch bridges can be prefabricated offsite, and subsequently floated, hauled or lifted into place. A notable case was the installation of the Fremont Bridge in Portland.

Tenmile Creek Bridge is a tied-arch bridge.

TORSION – A twisting force or action.

TRESTLE – A bridge structure consisting of spans supported upon frame bents.

TRUSS – A rigid, jointed structure made up of individual straight pieces arranged and connected, usually in a triangular pattern, so as to support longer spans.

TRUSS BRIDGE – A bridge having a pair of trusses for the superstructure.

Trusses on the Columbia River Bridge.

UNDERPASS – A bridge structure where the principal or subject transportation facility is the lower roadway (of two roadway levels).

VIADUCT – Usually a bridge built over dry land or a wide valley and consisting of a number of small spans. (Several structures along the Oregon Coast are called viaducts even though they cross waterways.)

UPPER CHORD – The top longitudinal member of a truss.

VERTICAL LIFT SPAN – A movable bridge which can be raised vertically by weights and pulleys operating in towers at each end of the structure. During raising and lowering, the bridge remains in a horizontal position.

Vertical lift span on Youngs Bay Bridge.

WARREN TRUSS – A triangular truss with sloping members (and no vertical members) between the top and bottom chords, forming the letter "W."

WEB – The portion of a beam located between and connected to the flanges.

WELDED JOINT – A joint in which the assembled elements and members are united through fusion of metal.

WROUGHT IRON – A comparatively pure form of iron, almost entirely free of carbon and having a fibrous structure that is readily forged and welded.

[With gratitude, used by permission of the Washington and Oregon Departments of Transportation.]

Bibliography

Stan Allyn. *Heave To! You'll Drown Yourselves!* Portland, OR: Binfords & Mort, 1982.

D. Alt and D.W. Hyndman. *Roadside Geology of Oregon.* Missoula, MT: Mountain Press Publishing Co., 1978.

Stephen E. Ambrose. *Undaunted Courage: Meriwether Lewis, Thomas Jefferson and the Opening of the American West.* New York: Touchstone/Simon & Schuster, 1996.

Stephen Dow Beckham. *Bandon-by-the-Sea: Hope and Perseverance in an Oregon Coastal Town.* Coos Bay, OR: Arago Books, 1990.

Stephen Dow Beckham. *The Simpsons of Shore Acres.* Coos Bay, OR: Arago Books, 1971.

David P. Billington. *The Tower and the Bridge: The New Are of Structural Engineering.* Princeton, NJ: Princeton University Press, 1983.

Joe R. Blakely. *Lifting Oregon out of the Mud.* Wallowa, OR: Bear Creek Press, 2006.

James E. Brooks, Editor. *The Oregon Almanac and Book of Facts 1961-1962.* Portland, OR: Binfords & Mort, 1961.

Bullard, Oral. 1968. *Crisis on the Columbia.* Portland, OR: Touchstone Press, 1968.

Ray Bottenberg. *Bridges of Portland.* Charleston, SC: Arcadia Publishing, 2007.

Darlene Castle, Brenda Eddleman, Meg Hughes, Riley Hughes, Paul Thompson. *Yaquina Bay 1878-1978.* Newport, OR: Lincoln County Historical Society; Waldport, OR: Oldtown Printers, 1979.

Thomas Condon. *The Two Islands and What Came of Them.* Portland, OR: J.K. Gill, 1902.

Edwin D. Culp. *Oregon: The Way It Was.* Caldwell, ID: The Caxton Printers, 1981.

Samuel N. Dicken and Emily F. Dicken. *The Making of Oregon: A Study in Historical Geography.* Portland, OR: Oregon Historical Society Press, 1979.

Gordon B. Dodds. *Oregon: A Bicentennial History.* New York: W.W. Norton & Company, Inc., 1977.

Nathan Douthit. *A Guide to Oregon South Coast History.* Coos Bay, OR: River West Books, 1986.

Nathan Douthit. *The Coos Bay Region, 1890-1944: Life on a Coastal Frontier.* Coos Bay, OR: River West Books, 1981.

Leonard C. Ekman. *Scenic Geology of the Pacific Northwest.* Portland, OR, Binfords & Mort, 1965.

Robert W. Hadlow. *Elegant Arches, Soaring Spans: C.B. McCullough, Oregon's Master Bridge Builder.* Corvallis, OR: Oregon State University Press, 2001.

David Freeman Hawke. *Those Tremendous Mountains: The Story of the Lewis and Clark Expedition.* New York: W.W. Norton, 1980.

Martin Hayden. *The Book of Bridges.* New York: Galahad Books, 1976.

Washington Irving. *Astoria.* New York: Putnam, 1890; Portland, OR: Binfords & Mort, 1950.

Dorothy O. Johansen and Charles Gates. *Empire of the Columbia: A History of the Pacific Northwest.* Harper & Row, New York, 1967.

George Kramer. *Slab, Beam & Girder Bridges in Oregon: Historic Context Statement.* Eugene, OR: Heritage Research Associates, 2004.

David Lavender. *The Way to the Western Sea: Lewis and Clark Across the Continent.* New York: Harper & Row, 1988.

D. Lee and J.H. Frost. *Ten Years in Oregon.* New York: J. Collard, 1844.

Lewis A. McArthur. *Oregon Geographic Names Fifth Edition.* Portland, OR: Oregon Historical Society Press, 1992.

David McCullough. *The Great Bridge: The Epic Story of the Building of the Brooklyn Bridge.* New York: Avon, 1972.

E. Kimbark MacColl and Harry H. Stein. *Merchants, Money, and Power: The Portland Establishment, 1843-1913.* Portland, OR: The Georgian Press, 1988.

Harold Avery Minter. *Umpqua Valley, Oregon and Its Pioneers*. Portland, OR, 1967.

Wallis Nash. *Oregon: There and Back in 1877*. Corvallis, OR: Oregon State University Press, 1976.

Earl M. Nelson, Editor. *Pioneer History of North Lincoln County, Oregon, Vol. 1*. McMinnville, OR: The Telephone Register Publishing Co., 1951.

Lee H. Nelson. A *Century of Oregon Covered Bridges, 1851-1952*. Portland, OR: Oregon Historical Society, 1960.

J. Richard Nokes. *Columbia's River: The Voyages of Robert Gray, 1787-1793*. Tacoma, WA: Washington State Historical Society, 1991.

James Norman. *Oregon Main Street: A Rephotographic Survey*. Portland, OR: Oregon Historical Society Press, 1994.

Terence O'Donnell. *Cannon Beach, A Place by the Sea*. Portland, OR: Oregon Historical Society Press, 1996.

Steven A. Ostrow. *Bridges*. New York: Metro Books, 1997.

Henry Petroski. *Engineers of Dreams: Great Builders and the Spanning of America*. New York: Vintage Books, 1995.

David Plowden. *Bridges The Spans of North America*. New York: W.W. Norton, 1974.

Richard Price. *Newport Oregon: 1866-1936, Portrait of a Coast Resort*. Dallas, OR: Itemizer-Observer, 1975.

Herman Francis Reinhart. *The Golden Frontier, The Recollections of Herman Francis Reinhart 1851-1869*. Austin, TX: University of Texas Press, 1962.

Dwight A. Smith, James B. Norman, and Pieter A. Dykman. *Historic Highway Bridges of Oregon*. Salem, OR: Oregon Department of Transportation, 1985.

David B. Steinman and Sara Ruth Wilson. *Bridges and Their Builders*. New York: Dover Publications, 1957.

J.E. Stembridge, Editor. *Pathfinder, The First Automobile Trip From Newport to Siletz Bay, Oregon July, 1912*. Newport, OR: Lincoln County Historical Society, 1975.

Kathryn A. Straton. *Oregon's Beaches: A Birthright Preserved*. Salem, OR: Oregon State Parks and Recreation Branch, 1977.

Jerry Winterbotham. *Umpqua: The Lost County of Oregon*. Brownsville, OR: Creative Images Printing, 1994.

Sharon Wood Wortman with Ed Wortman. *The Portland Bridge Book*. Portland, OR, Urban Adventure Press, 1999.

Work Projects Administration. *Oregon: End of the Trail*. Portland, OR: Oregon State Board of Control and Binfords & Mort, 1940.

Bridge Notes

Columbia River (Astoria) Bridge

1. Designed by Conde B. McCullough, the Rogue River Bridge was financed and constructed under President Herbert Hoover's Reconstruction Finance Corporation. McCullough also designed the five major bridges funded by Franklin D. Roosevelt's Public Works Administration, constructed in 1934-36. Often referred to as the Oregon Coast Bridges Project, they included Yaquina Bay, Siuslaw River, Alsea Bay, Umpqua River, and Coos Bay. The original Alsea Bay Bridge was replaced in 1991. For an overview of the PWA see **http://bluebook.state.or.us/facts/scenic/dep/depintro.htm**

2. Astoria Bridge Dedication Program, Oregon Department of Transportation, (Salem, OR), August 27, 1966. The Dedication Program includes information on the $24 million dollar cost of the bridge and the interstate agreement between Oregon and Washington. Regarding the cost of the Oregon Coast Highway, a 1943 Oregon Department of Transportation memo, "Oregon Coast Highway," puts the total Oregon Coast Highway cost between 1917 and 1942 at $24,900,000, of which $15,064,000 were state funds, $2,044,000 county, and $7,748,000 federal. Regarding these costs, I also reference a speech by Oregon State Highway Commission chairman Leslie Scott at the opening of the Rogue River Bridge and the Oregon Coast Highway. See Leslie Scott, "Oregon Coast Highway," *Oregon Historical Quarterly*, No. 33 (1932), 268.

3. Oregon Department of Transportation pamphlet *The Astoria-Megler Bridge from "the bridge to nowhere," to… Astoria's Bridge to the World,* (Salem, OR: Oregon Department of Transportation, 1993).

4. Astoria Bridge Dedication Program, Oregon Department of Transportation, (Salem, OR), August 27, 1966.

   For more about Gray's discovery see Dorothy O. Johansen, *Empire of the Columbia* (New York: Harper and Row, 1967), 52-58.

5. "Great Span at Astoria Considered," *Oregon Journal*, January 16, 1928.

6. "An Economic Analysis of Short-span Suspension Bridges for Modern Highway Loadings," *Technical Bulletin No. 11,* (Salem, Oregon, Oregon State Highway Commission), 1938.

7. *The Astoria-Megler Bridge from "the bridge to nowhere," to… Astoria's Bridge to the World.*

8. "Report on Trans-Columbia River Interstate Bridge Studies," *Technical Bulletin No. 16,* (Salem, Oregon, Oregon State Highway Commission), 1944.

9. Oregon Department of Transportation pamphlet, *The Astoria-Megler Bridge from "the bridge to nowhere" to…Astoria's Bridge to the World.* (Salem, OR: Oregon Department of Transportation, 1993).

10. Astoria Bridge Dedication Program, Oregon Department of Transportation, (Salem, OR), August 27, 1966.

11. Ibid.

12. Oregon Department of Transportation pamphlet, *The Astoria-Megler Bridge from "the bridge to nowhere" to…Astoria's Bridge to the World.* (Salem, OR: Oregon Department of Transportation, 1993).

13. Brian S. Akre, "Critics of Astoria Bridge Silenced by its Success," *The Oregonian* (Portland, OR), July 21, 1986.

14. Ibid.

15. Oregon Department of Transportation pamphlet, *The Astoria-Megler Bridge from "the bridge to nowhere" to…Astoria's Bridge to the World.* (Salem, OR: Oregon Department of Transportation, 1993).

Youngs Bay Bridge

1. "Span Dedicated, Queen Crowned At Astoria," *The Sunday Oregonian* (Portland, OR), Aug. 30, 1964.

2. Interview with John Discasey, ODOT Region One drawbridge tender, 06/19/2010.

3. Lewis A. McArthur, *Oregon Geographic Names, 5th ed.* (Portland, OR: Western Imprints, The Press of the Oregon Historical Society 1982), 819.

Old Youngs Bay Bridge

1. C.B. McCullough letter to J.C. Ainsworth, 23 November 1922, copy held by author.

Lewis and Clark River Bridge

1. Dwight A. Smith, James B. Norman, and Pieter Dykman, *Historic Highway Bridges of Oregon* (Salem: Oregon Department of Transportation, 1985), 288.

Neawanna Creek Bridge

1. Michael Goff, "Historic American Buildings Survey/Historic American Engineering Record/Historic American Landscapes Survey," http://hdl.loc.gov/loc.pnp/hhh.or0508.

2. Richard G. Weingardt, "Hardy Cross A Man Ahead of His Time," *STRUCTURE magazine,* March 2005, 40-41.

Necanicum River (Seaside) Bridge

1. Dwight A. Smith et al., *Historic Highway Bridges of Oregon,* 97.

2. "Engineer sues contractor," *The Oregonian,* November 26, 1931, 9.

3. Dwight A. Smith et al., *Historic Highway Bridges of Oregon,* 97.

4. Interview with Al Harwood, Project Engineer, Public Works and Engineering Department, City of Seaside, 26 September, 2000.

    City of Seaside memorandum to Improvement Commission members, from Larry Lehman, Administrative Officer, 17 December, 1992.

5. Terrance O'Donnell, *Cannon Beach, A Place by the Sea* (Portland, OR: Oregon Historical Society Press, 1996), 14.

Necarney Creek (Samuel G. Reed) Bridge

1. Samuel Herbert Boardman, "Oregon State Park System: A Brief History," *Oregon Historical Quarterly*, No. 55 (1954): 183-185.

Chasm (Neahkahnie Mountain) Bridge

1. Richard Engeman, "Highway 101, Neahakahnie Mountain," *The Oregon History Project,* Oregon Historical Society, 2005.

2. A series of articles by Bob McCain of the *Nehalem Bay News* in 1994 describe the landslides that closed US 101 over Neahkahnie Mountain. Bob McCain, "Huge Boulder Caused Hwy 101 Damage," *Nehalem Bay News* (Nehalem, OR, March 1994), 1. Bob McCain, "*Nehalem Bay News* (Nehalem, OR, May 1994), 1. Bob McCain, "*Nehalem Bay News* (Nehalem, OR, November, 1994), 1.

3. Lewis A. McArthur, *Oregon Geographic Names, 5th ed.* (Portland: Oregon Historical Society, 1982), 534. See also William L. Sullivan, *Hiking Oregon's History* (Eugene, OR, Navillus, 1999), 50-53.

    For an overview of the WPA see ***http://bluebook.state.or.us/facts/scenic/dep/depintro.htm***

Wilson River Bridge

1. Lewis A. McArthur, *Oregon Geographic Names,* 5th ed. (Portland: Oregon Historical Society, 1982), 803.

2. Robert W. Hadlow, *Historic American Engineering Record*, Oregon Bridges Project, Summer 1990, Preliminary Drawings and Draft Narratives, October 1990, 136.

3. Ibid, 136-139.

West Beaver Creek Bridge

1. Supplementary Bridge Inspection and Maintenance Report, Oregon State Highway Commission – Bridge Department, 21 June, 1939.

Drift Creek Bridge (Restored site on Bear Creek)

1. Dwight A. Smith et al., *Historic Highway Bridges of Oregon,* 164.

2. "Drift Creek (Bear Creek) Covered Bridge," Oregon.com, http://***www.oregon.com/covered_bridges/drift_ck; see also http://web. oregon.com/covered_bridges/bridges/bear_creek.cfm***

3. Laura Mitchell Sweitz, *The Story of the Drift Creek Covered Bridge* (flyer at bridge site).

4. Steve Wyatt, "UPDATE! Drift Creek Bridge is gone!" http://home. comcast.net/~draft10/bridges/drift-cr.html.

Siletz River Bridge

1. "Siletz River's future debated at Coast Guard Kernville Bridge hearing," *The News Guard* (Lincoln City, OR), Jan. 28, 1971.

2. "New Siletz support builds from planners, legislators," *The News Guard* (Lincoln City, OR), Dec. 17, 1970.

3. Lewis A. McArthur, *Oregon Geographic Names*, 411-12.

4. Anne Hall, "Once there was a town called Kernville" (from *Out of the Past,* a Lincoln County Historical Society pamphlet).

5. Larry King, "Movie Star House*," Oregon Coast,* July/August 1991. An interesting article that describes the house as originally constructed for the film and details improvements subsequent owners made to turn the original structure into a permanent home.

Depoe Bay Bridge

1. "Depoe Bay," *Lincoln County Herald*, Jan. 6, 1927. (Copy in author's possession)

2. Oregon State Highway Department, *14th Biennial Report, 1939-40.* (Salem, OR: State of Oregon, 115.)

3. ODOT document A-8, Depoe Bay Arch (Depoe Bay Bridge), located in Bridge Section Historic Bridge Files.

4. Lewis A. McArthur, *Oregon Geographic Names*, 216-17.

Rocky Creek (Ben F. Jones) Bridge

1. Dianne Sichel, "Salt Problem May Mean End To Old Span," *Oregon Journal* (Portland, OR), July 28, 1973.

2. Rehabilitation report: ***http://cms.cityoftacoma.org/CRO/2%/20d.pdf***

Spencer Creek (Beverly Beach) Bridge

1. ***http://www.oregon.gov/ODOT/HWY/REGION2/spencer_creek.shtml***

2. Lewis A. McArthur, *Oregon Geographic Names*, 59.

Yaquina Bay (Newport) Bridge

1. Conde B. McCullough and R.A. Furrow, "Yaquina Bay Bridge," *The Oregon Motorist,* May 1936, 11.

2. R.H. Baldock, "Bridge builders' secrets," *The Oregon Motorist*, May 1936, 5.

3. Conde B. McCullough letter to Mr. Aymar Embury II dated May 6, 1938. Copy in author's possession.

4. M.E. Reed, "Building the Yaquina Bay Bridge On the Oregon Coast Highway," *Western Construction News* (San Francisco, CA), May 1936, 133.

5. Though not officially a part of US 101, a ferry did operate across the Coquille River at Bullards, connecting the south end of the Seven Devils Road with Bandon until 1962. The ferry was displaced by the opening of the Coquille River (Bullards) Bridge, when US 101 was rerouted connecting Bandon and Coos Bay directly, rather than

going inland through the county seat of Coquille, shortening the route by about 20 miles (See Coquille River (Bullards) Bridge.)

6. Darlene Castle et al., *Yaquina Bay, 1778-1978* (Waldport, OR: Old Town Printers, 1978), 55.

7. Ibid, 56.

8. Don and Inez Klopfenstein, "Yaquina Bay Bridge Gets First Facelift in 40 Years," *Pacific Builder and Engineer,* (Aug. 18, 1980), 16-18.

9. Carmel Finley, "New Plan to Expand Life of Coast Spans," *The Oregonian* (Portland, OR), Nov. 16, 1992.

10. Byron H. Dudley, "Rediscover 'New Albion,'" *Oregon Coast,* December/January 1983, 46-7.

11. *Yaquina Bay 1778-1978*, 4.

12. Richard L. Price, *Newport, Oregon: 1866-1936* (Newport, OR: Lincoln County Historical Society, 1975), 10.

13. *Yaquina Bay* 1778-1978, 5-10.

14. Oregon History, http://web.oregon.com/history/hm/grand_ronde.cfm, The Oregon Interactive Corporation, 2006.

15. Oregon History Project, ***www.orhist@ohs.org***, Oregon Historical Society, 2002.

16. Oregon History, http://web.oregon.com/history/hm/grand_ronde.cfm, The Oregon Interactive Corporation, 2006.

17. Richard L. Price, *Newport, Oregon*, 7.

Alsea Bay (Waldport) Bridge

1. Carmel Finley, "Old—and new—Bridges Honored," *Statesman Journal* (Salem, OR), Aug. 25, 1991.

2. Larry Bacon, "Waldport Dedicates New Bay Bridge," *Eugene Register Guard* (Eugene, OR), August 25, 1991, 1C.

3. Ibid, 2C.

4. "Waldport sets party for bridge," *Eugene Register Guard,* August 23, 1991.

Cooks Chasm Bridge

1. Vibia Perpetua was executed in the arena in Carthage on 7 March 203. The account of her martyrdom, technically a Passion, is apparently historical and has special interest as much of it was written in Latin by Perpetua herself before her death. This makes it one of the earliest pieces of writing by a Christian woman. It is unclear why Cook named this site for Perpetua. See the *Internet Medieval Sourcebook* ed. by Paul Halsall (1996): ***http://www.fordham.edu/halsall/sbook.html***.

Cummins Creek Bridge

1. Lewis A. McArthur, *Oregon Geographic Names,* 200.

2. Dwight A. Smith et al., *Historic Highway Bridges of Oregon,* 283.

Big Creek Bridge

1. Big Creek Bridge: Revised Environmental Assessment, Federal Highway Administration, September 1996.

2. See p. 89 for difference between original "X" portal bracing and "lazy K bracing. Also see p. 92 photo for original "X" portal bracing and p. 181 portal photo in Glossary for "Lazy K' bracing.

Cape Creek Bridge

1. Historic American Engineering Record (HAER), Oregon Bridges Project, Summer 1990, Preliminary Drawings and Draft Narratives, 177-192.

2. Robert W. Hadlow, *Elegant Arches, Soaring Spans,* (Corvallis, OR: OSU Press, 2001), 85-86.

3. HAER, 184-187.

4. Larry Bacon, "Electric charge to preserve historic Cape Creek Bridge, *Eugene Register Guard,* (Eugene, OR), 7/4/1989.

Siuslaw River (Florence) Bridge

1. C[onde]. B. McCullough, "Siuslaw River Bridge," *The Oregon Motorist,* (Portland, OR: May 1936), 8.

2. Lewis A. McArthur, *Oregon Geographic Names*, Oregon Historical Society Press, 1982, 280.

Smith River Bridge, Bolon Island Cut, and Umpqua River Bridge

Smith River Bridge

1. C.B. McCullough, D.R. Smith, L.L. Jensen, "Umpqua River Bridge," *The Oregon Motorist*, (Portland, OR, Oregon State Motorist Association, Vol. XVI, No. 4, May 1936,) 8.

2. R[obert] H. Baldock, "Bridge Builders' Secrets," *The Oregon Motorist*, (Portland, OR, Oregon State Motorist Association, Vol. XVI, No. 4, May 1936), 5-6.

3. Nathan Douthit, *A Guide to Oregon South Coast History: Traveling the Jedediah Smith Trail* (Coos Bay, OR: River West Books, 1986), 117-119.

   Also see Dorothy Johansen, *Empire of the Columbia: A History of the Pacific Northwest*, Second Edition (New York: Harper and Row, 1967), 138-39.

Umpqua River Bridge

1. Robert W. Hadlow, *Elegant Arches, Soaring Spans* (Corvallis, OR: Oregon State University Press, 2001), 107.

   The Coquille River Bridge, bypassed in 1986, was offered free to anyone who could find another home for it. No one did, so it was cut up and sold for scrap in the early 1980s. See Bill Calder, "At this price, historic bridge a giveaway," *The Oregonian*, August 18, 1989.

2. Nathan Douthit, *A Guide to Oregon South Coast History: Traveling the Jedediah Smith Trail* (Corvallis, OR: Oregon State University Press, 1986), 56.

Coos Bay (Conde B. McCullough) Bridge

1. Conde B. McCullough letter to Aymar Embry II.

2. See Robert W. Hadlow, *Elegant Arches, Soaring Spans,* for a description and photographs of McCullough's suspension bridges in Central America.

3. Historic American Engineering Record (HAER), Oregon Bridges Project, Summer 1990, Preliminary Drawings and Draft Narratives, 177-192.

4. Cheryl Landes, "McCullough Bridge, Engineering as Art", *Oregon Coast,* July/August 1991, 22-23.

5. A.O. Chase, "Design of Coast Highway Bridges," *Civil Engineering,* October 1936, 648.

6. *Coos Bay Times, Bridge Jubilee Edition,* June 5th-7th, 1936.

7. Dick and Judy Wagner, *North Bend Between The World Wars: 1919-1941*, (North Bend, OR 2005, Bygones), 54-57.

8. "U.S. 101 Bridge Over Coos Bay Closed After Ship Hits Span," *The Oregonian* (Portland, OR), December 5, 1986, D6.

Coquille River (Bullards) Bridge

1. Nathan Douthit, *A Guide to Oregon South Coast History: Traveling the Jedediah Smith Trail* (River West Books, Coos Bay, OR, 1986), 63.

2. Ibid., 65.

3. Nathan Douthit, *The Coos Bay Region 1890-1944: Life on a Coastal Frontier* (Coos Bay: River West Books, 1981), 75.

4. R.H. [B]aldock (sic), State Highway Engineer, to The District Engineer, Corps of Engineers, U.S. Army, November 13, 1950. One of many communications between the Oregon State Highway Commission and other agencies, especially Coos County, regarding the construction of the Coquille River (Bullards) Bridge north of Bandon. Constructed in 1952, the bridge became an integral part of US 101 in 1960.

5. Nathan Douthit, *A Guide to Oregon South Coast History,* 64.

Reinhart Creek Bridge

1. Lewis A. McArthur, *Oregon Geographic Names*, 617-18.

2. Herman Reinhart, *The Golden Frontier: The Recollections of Herman Francis Reinhart 1851-1869* (Austin: University of Texas Press, 1962), Epilogue.

Euchre Creek (Orphir Road) Bridge

1. Dwight A. Smith et al., *Historic Highway Bridges of Oregon*, 293.

Rogue River (Isaac Lee Patterson) Bridge

1. Oregon State Highway Commission, *9th Biennial Report, 1928-30*. (Salem, OR: State of Oregon), 288.

2. Nathan Douthit, *A Guide to Oregon South Coast History: Traveling the Jedediah Smith Trail* (Corvallis, OR: Oregon State University Press, 1999), 56-57.

3. Robert Withrow, to Conde B. McCullough, OSHD, April, 26, 1932.

4. A.W. Norblad, to Leslie M. Scott, Oregon State Highway Commission, March 31, 1932.

5. Oregon State Highway Commission to A.W. Norblad, April 14, 1932.

6. "Great Throng Joins in Big Celebration," *Curry County Reporter* (Gold Beach, OR), June 2, 1932.

7. Thomas T. Thalken, Director, National Archives and Records Service, Herbert Hoover Presidential Library, to Ray A. Allen, September 12, 1980.

8, "Great Throng Joins in Big Celebration," *Curry County Reporter*, June 2, 1932.

9. Dale C. Mayer, Archivist, National Archives and Records Service, Herbert Hoover Presidential Library, to Ray A. Allen, October 6, 1980. Mayer quotes the *U.S. Daily*, a Washington, D.C. newspaper that tracked White House appointments, showing that the president did visit the White House at 3:45 PM for an unspecified purpose on the day in question.

10. Conde B. McCullough, "Oregon Coast Highway Bridges, Resume of Traffic Studies, Revenue Expectations and Toll Requirements," ODOT document, 1935. Copy in possession of author.

11. Albin L. Gemeny and Conde B. McCullough, *Application of Freyssinet Method of Concrete Arch Construction to the Rogue River Bridge in Oregon: A Cooperative Research Project* (Salem, OR: Oregon State Highway Commission, April 1933).

12. Emil R. Peterson and Alfred Powers, *A Century of Coos and Curry: History of Southwest Oregon* (Portland, OR: Binfords and Mort for Coos-Curry Pioneer and Historical Association, 1952), 440-41.

13. Letter from Mrs. C.J. Edwards for Coos Bay Chapter, D.A.R., Marshfield, OR to Oregon State Highway Commission dated Jan 15, 1932.

Thomas Creek Bridge

1. Rodger Hoyt, "The Screaming Bridge," *Oregon Coast* 10, no. 4, July/August 1991, 16.

2. "Coastal Bridge Built From 'Top Down,'" *Portland Reporter*, June 24, 1961, 3M.

3. Rodger Hoyt, "The Screaming Bridge."

Chetco River (Benjamin A. Martin) Bridge

1. Prestressed Concrete Institute quoted in the Oregon State Highway Division *Biennial Report, 1973-74*. (Salem, OR: State of Oregon), 43.

2. "Bridges of the Chetco River," *Brookings-Harbor Pilot*, September, 21, 1972.

3. Oregon State Highway Division, *"News Release,"* Public Information Office, Salem, Oregon, September 12, 1972.

Oregon Coast Highway Notes

1. Oswald West, *2nd Biennial Report*, Oregon State Highway Commission, 1916.

2. See William A. Brakken, "Oswald West and Oregon's Beaches," *Oregon Coast* 12, no. 2, March/April 1993, for a comprehensive analysis of West's motives for making the beaches a highway

3. See Kathryn A. Straton, *Oregon's Beaches: A Birthright Preserved* (Salem, OR: Oregon State Parks and Recreation Branch, 1977), 3, for quotes from Lewis and Clark journals regarding using the beach as a highway. Also provides a complete assessment of the Oregon Beach Bill.

4. J.E. Turnbull, "The Oregon Coast Highway Route One Hundred Years Ago," *The Oregon Motorist*, December 1932, 5-18. See also Nathan Douthit, *A Guide to Oregon South Coast History*, (Coos Bay, Oregon, River West Books, 1986.)

5. Nathan Douthit, *A Guide to Oregon South Coast History*, 123.

6. Terence O'Donnell, *Cannon Beach: A Place by the Sea* (Portland, OR: Oregon Historical Society Press, 1996), 24-25.

7. Nathan Douthit, *A Guide to Oregon South Coast History*, 21. See also Stephen Dow Beckham, *Coos Bay: The Pioneer Period 1851-1890* (Coos Bay, OR: Arago Books, 1973).

8. Emil R. Peterson and Alfred Powers, *A Century of Coos and Curry County, History of Southwest Oregon,* (Portland, OR, Binfords and Mort, 1952), 480.

9. Samuel N. Dicken and Emily F. Dicken, *The Making of Oregon, A Study in Historical Geography* (Portland: Oregon Historical Society Press, 1979), 115.

10. Darlene Castle et al., *Yaquina Bay 1778-1978,* 14.

11. Oswald West's Inaugural Address as the 14th Governor of Oregon, Oregon State Archives. http://arcweb.sos.state.or.us/governors/west/inaugural1911.html

12. James E. Stembridge, ed., *Pathfinder, The First Automobile Trip From Newport To Siletz Bay, Oregon, July, 1912* (Newport, OR: Lincoln County Historical Society, 1975).

13. Gary Meier, "When The Highway Was Sand," *Oregon Coast*, January/February 1991, 27-29. See also *Standard Oil Bulletin* article, 1916, adapted by Coos County Historical Society Newsletter.

14. "Big Coast Loop is Put into Existence by 11-Mile Highway," *The Oregonian*, August 27, 1916, Section 2, 8.

15. "G.F. Beck Praises Coast Road South," *The Sunday Oregonian*, July 23, 1916, Section 4, 6.

Snow north of Coos Bay Bridge, 1949.

16. Samuel N. Dicken and Emily F. Dicken, *The Making of Oregon, A Study in Historical Geography* (Portland: Oregon Historical Society Press, 1979), 140.

17. Samuel N. Dicken et al., 96. See also E. I. Cantine, "Second Annual Report of the engineer of the Oregon State Highway Commission for the year ending November 30, 1915," Salem, OR, 13.

18. The National Archives, "Teaching with Documents: The Zimmermann Telegram," ***http://www.archives.gov/education/lessons/zimmermann/***

19. "I. S. Smith Was Among First to Vision Highway," *Coos Bay Times*, Marshfield and North Bend, Oregon, June 5th-7th, 1936.

20. James Withycombe, 1915 Inaugural Speech and 1917 Address to the Legislature. Oregon State Archives. Although not mentioned directly in these speeches, the

Oregon Coast Highway was included in the statewide highway plan endorsed by Withycombe.

21. W.S. Chiene, "Conquest of Oregon's Coast," *The Oregon Motorist*, May 1936, 16. Over the years in various publications, Ben Jones is referred to as "Father of the Roosevelt Coast Military Highway," "Father of the Roosevelt Coast Highway," and "Father of the Oregon Coast Highway."

22. Emil B. Peterson et al., 572.

23. Oregon State Highway Commission, *6th Biennial Report*, 1923-1924, 55-6.

24. Lawrence Barber, "58 Years Ago, Daring Drivers Took to Roosevelt Coast Highway," *The Oregonian* (Portland, OR), October, 25, 1987.

25. Samuel N. Dicken et al., 140-143.

26. Leslie Scott, "*Oregon Coast Highway*," *Oregon Historical Quarterly*, Vol. 33, No. 3, September 1932, 268-270.

27. Oregon State Highway Commission, *9th Biennial Report*, 1928-1930, 13-14.

28. Robert W. Hadlow, *Elegant Arches, Soaring Spans,* 89.

29. Ibid, 22-25.

30. For more complete information on Thomas H. MacDonald, his role as director of the Bureau of Public Roads, and connection with Conde B. McCullough, see Robert W. Hadlow, *Elegant Arches, Soaring Spans,* especially pages 35-36 and 46-47.

Driver on highway roller in the early 1940s.

Conde B. McCullough

E. Shellin Atly, *C.B. McCullough and the Oregon Coastal Bridges Project,* 1977.

Bill Calder, "Conde Balcom McCullough: Oregon's Master Bridge Builder." *Oregon Coast* (June/July 1986).

Robert W. Hadlow, "C.B. McCullough: The Engineer and Oregon's Bridge-Building Boom, 1919-1936." *Pacific Northwest Quarterly* 82, no. 1 (January 1991).

Robert W. Hadlow, "Conde Balcomb McCullough: Oregon's Bridge Builder."

Oregon Historic Bridges Recording Project (Summer 1990).

Robert W. Hadlow, *Elegant Arches, Soaring Spans.* Corvallis, Oregon State University Press, 2001.

Lynda Leary, "Bridge Builder Conde McCullough." *Oregon Coast* (July/August 1991).

Louis F. Pierce, "C.B. McCullough, Structural Artist in Bridges." Oregon Department of Transportation, 1987.

Louis F. Pierce, "Esthetics In Oregon Bridges—McCullough To Date." (Preprint for the ASCE Convention and Exposition, Portland, OR, April 14-18, 1980).

ACKNOWLEDGEMENTS

Many people contributed to this book, several in important ways. My wife Denise shared that joyous day when seeing the old Alsea Bay Bridge again inspired me to write a book about the Oregon Coast bridges. My partner when I began researching the book, as it came to life she became my most steadfast supporter, nag, and critic. Her extraordinary vocabulary and instincts about word usage served me time and again, and her upbeat morale through some pretty trying times still amazes me. As the book became our third child, whose rearing tested the boundaries of reasonable time limits, she pronounced the loving sentiment that finally became a reality: "Get it done!"

As the book concept developed, my passion for bridges far exceeded my knowledge. To learn, I sought out people who knew about Oregon's historic bridges and shared my concern about their preservation. Dwight Smith, then cultural resource specialist for the Oregon Department of Transportation (ODOT), answered my call. Principal author of *Historic Highway Bridges of Oregon*, Dwight supported my efforts to save the old Alsea Bay Bridge, reviewed an early draft of my manuscript, and continues to provide valuable guidance as I write this. He also indulged me by writing my *Foreword*.

More recently James Norman, another long-time ODOT colleague, co-author, designer, and photographer of *Historic Highway Bridges of Oregon*, author of several of his own books and producer of others, reinvigorated my publishing plans. His wisdom, encouragement, and technical skill showed me the path to publish my book. He and Mark Falby, our graphics guru, designed and produced the book.

Much gratitude and credit go to my editor Sharon Franklin, who helped make order out of chaos and clarity out of confusion. Beyond editorial contributions, her friendship and passion for this project provided a special bonus. Likewise, I'm indebted to Douglas Foran, whose early enthusiastic and creative review of my manuscript gave me ideas that are seen in the text. Their efforts greatly improved the quality of the book.

I'm most appreciative to Robert Hadlow for his thoughtful and thorough critiques of my manuscript. Author of *Elegant Arches, Soaring Spans,* a Conde B. McCullough biography, Bob's comprehensive knowledge of McCullough and the Oregon coast bridges made his input incomparable.

I also want to acknowledge several other ODOT employees who helped me over the years. People like Maxine Banks and Elizabeth Potter who aided me in my research, but whom I most remember for their steadfast support in my effort to save the old Alsea Bay Bridge. Maxine didn't live to see this book published, but her comforting spirit lives within its pages. Another, Pieter Dykman, then Environmental Unit manager and co-author of *Historic Bridges of Oregon,* always fair-minded and friendly, embraced me like an insider, which I consider a great compliment.

George Bell, ODOT's former assistant director for intergovernmental relations, listened to and supported my interest in preserving the Oregon Coast Highway and bridges before it became fashionable. He opened an opportunity for me to make my case to then ODOT director Fred Miller and chief bridge engineer Walter Hart. While they didn't immediately champion my cause, in the end they were supportive and helpful.

Special thanks to John Discasey, Leroy Morrell, and the other ODOT drawbridge tenders who work the bridges around Astoria's Youngs Bay, who went out of their way to show me their world. They, like other maintenance crews along the coast and across Oregon, keep us motorists moving, but are rarely rewarded. I love these guys.

And where would any writer be without those helpful librarians and archivists? In my case assistance I got early on from ODOT librarians Faith Steffen and Garnet Elliott helped me define the scope of the book. I especially thank archivist Carolyn Philp for her generous assistance in accessing bridge files and other archival records. More recently, I want to thank librarian Laura Wilt, whose thoughtful support helped me discover hidden resources, and Patricia Solomon, archivist of ODOT's History Center. For the other unnamed librarians, historical society staff, and volunteers who assisted me in my research over the years, you have my eternal gratitude. Your services are invaluable to those of us who mine historical treasures.

The Yaquina Bay Bridge in a view looking south.

Appreciation goes to my son Aaron Allen and friend Hope Benedict for their helpful critiques of an early draft of the book. No one was more astonished and thrilled than Aaron when he got the news that my book was going to be published. My other son, Cooper Allen, shared his rearing with this book. When he was little he often sat with me evenings as I worked on the book, sometimes drawing pictures of the bridges. Like his mother, his patience often ran out and at those times would ask, "Dad, when are you going to finish this book?"

Thanks to my late parents, Odie Ray Allen and Edith Ayers Allen for their undying support. As a Navy brat, my early peripatetic life exposed me to the phenomenal cultural diversity that has become America's trademark. Their sense of social justice, fairness, and respect for others has served me well.

My dad was my greatest fan. He ferried me and my friends on countless outings and camping excursions and faithfully followed my athletic career into college. My mother, a teacher with a more literary bent, taught me that books were my friends, advice that has comforted me during the thirty years I've lived with this one.

To my sisters Anita Oderman and Natalie Allen, and their spouses, Dale Oderman and Scott Tibbling, my gratitude for their continuing love and support. I want especially to acknowledge my late sister Edith Allen, with whom I shared so many life adventures, especially those early ones at my grandparents' cabin on Heceta Beach.

I was blessed to be worked over for thirteen wonderful years by my furry friend Saki, "the smartest dog in the world," with whom I spent many coastal and other adventures. He came from Manzanita on the north coast, and I shared his last beach visit on an early Bandon morning. He's always with me, still.

With affection I want to salute my old Eugene cronies who remind me at each of our high school reunions that there is no substitute for old friends. My oldest friend, Jim Coleman and his wife Mary, opened their home and provided safe harbor during my marathon editing sessions in Eugene. They, along with another old crony, Charles "Nipper" Rhoads, and The Keg Tavern regulars, provided conversation, friendship, and a lot of cheer during my visits to Eugene.

Regards also to my Portland Community College colleagues, with whom I happily share my daily chores, especially Kathy Krug, and she knows why. Although he'll be surprised to know it, when family, work, and graduate school demands bogged me down, Glenn Harding, author of a couple of books himself, helped get me back on track by exhorting me with what later became Nike's motto: "Just do it." And so I did. Angie Blackwell, former council member of the Confederated Tribes of the Grand Ronde, helped to clarify the complicated origins of the Grand Ronde and Siletz reservations.

Finally, some special thanks to special friends for their years of support and encouragement. Our dear friends Margaret and Willie Gorrissen hosted us so many times their home seemed a destination resort. Melissa Dodworth, our enduring friend from Boise, often serves as a literary resource. To Mark and Kathy Bazeghi, with whom my wife and I have shared many trips, triumphs, and trials, what's next? And mostly, to our dearest friends, family really, Donald and Marjorie Farness, who live a stone's throw from Rocky Creek Bridge. We've been privileged to share their legendary hospitality with countless others. They gave beyond reason when we had need and, along with David McNutt and Nancy Kem, helped keep the embers glowing.

Biographies

Ray Allen *(Author)* grew up in Eugene, graduated from South Eugene High School and the University of Oregon, after an early childhood traveling the country as a Navy brat. He came to know many of the Oregon coast bridges as a child while visiting his grandparents who lived on Heceta Beach, outside Florence. A longtime preservationist, he helped lead a statewide effort to save the old Alsea Bay Bridge. He currently resides in Portland where he is a Career Advisor at Portland Community College.

James Norman *(Lead Photographer)* is an architectural photographer and historian, and is the Cultural Resources Manager for the Oregon Department of Transportation. He has documented more than 100 of Oregon's most significant historic resources for the Historic American Engineering Record (HAER) and the Historic American Building Survey (HABS), and was the official photographer for the 1999 HAER/NPS Willamette River Bridges Recordation Project and for the National Historic Landmark nomination for the Oregon Coast Bridges. He has authored several books on Oregon's architectural and engineering heritage, including the seminal *Historic Highway Bridges of Oregon* (ODOT 1985, OHS 1989 (2nd ed)), *Portland's Architectural Heritage* (OHS 1986), *Oregon Covered Bridges: A Study for the 1989-90 Oregon Legislature* (ODOT 1988), and *Oregon Main Street: A Rephotographic Survey* (OHS 1994). He also served as principal photographer and producer of the third edition of *The Portland Bridge Book* (Urban Adventures Press, 2006) by Sharon Wood Wortman. Mr. Norman's documentary photography has been widely published, and is included in the permanent collections of the Oregon Historical Society, the Smithsonian Institute and the Library of Congress. His fine art photography is included in the permanent collections of the Portland Art Museum and the Seattle Art Museum.

Mark A. Falby *(Publication Designer),* is a Publication Design Specialist for the Oregon Department of Transportation and provides graphics, illustrations, and layout services to ODOT and other state agencies. His work on the *Oregon Bike Plan* won national attention, with his illustrations shared with other publications nationwide. His work on the *Columbia River Gorge Bike Map* won a national publication award. He also served as Publication Designer of the third edition of *The Portland Bridge Book* (Urban Adventures Press, 2006) by Sharon Wood Wortman. He graduated with a B.F.A. in Fine Arts from the University of Oregon, and a Master of Art Education from Western Oregon State College.

Construction along the Oregon Coast Highway between Houser and Coos Bay with the new Coos Bay Bridge in the background.

Illustration Sources
Photography Credits

T = Top, L = Left, TL = Top Left, TR = Top Right, C = Center, CL = Center Left, CR = Center Right, B = Bottom, BR = Bottom Right

Ray Allen (author): xi and xii (from author's collection), 44, 68B, 69R, 72R, 104R, 105L, 124, 126T/B, 128, 144, 194, 195

> p. 164: Author's collection, courtesy of the Lincoln County Pioneer Museum

Tod Croteau for HAER: vii

Mark A. Falby (collection): 69L, 102T, 120R, 140B

Wanda Gifford (Oregon State University Archives): rear cover

Richard Koochagian for HAER: vii

Jet Lowe for HAER: xii, xiii, 39, 41, 54, 78, 104L, 110, 142, 143, 176, 181

James Norman for HAER: front cover, frontispiece, 2, 16, 17, 19, 20, 21, 22, 46, 47, 52, 56, 59, 64, 71, 73, 74, 79, 89T/B, 90, 91, 92, 94, 97, 100, 105R, 108, 109, 116, 122, 123,

Historic view of Neahakahnie Mountain at Chasm Bridge on the Oregon Coast Highway.

James Norman: 1, 4, 9, 12, 24, 25, 26, 27, 28, 30, 32, 33, 34, 35, 37, 38, 42, 48, 50, 60, 62, 63, 80, 82, 84, 85, 86, 87, 88, 106, 114, 132, 134, 136, 138, 141T/B, 147, 148, 150, 152, 154, 166, 179, 180, 181R, 182L,182C, 182R

Jedediah Smith Society: 157

North Lincoln County Historical Society: 51

ODOT: Dedication, 7, 8, 10T/B, 11, 14, 18, 31, 36, 53, 55, 58, 66, 67T/B, 72L, 75, 76, 77, 83, 96, 98, 99, 102B, 103, 105 C, 111, 112, 119, 120L, 121, 127, 130, 140T, 146, 149, 155, 158, 162L, 162R, 163, 165, 167, 168, 172, 173, 174, 175, 181C, 191, 192, 196, 197, 198

p. 159: Oregon Department of Transportation History Center. Original negatives of the Pathfinder expedition—possibly by Fred F. Sassman—are included in the William H. Burton photograph collection, PH006, Special Collections & University Archives, University of Oregon Libraries.

Oregon State Highway Commission: 160; 161

Thomas Robinson (Historic Photo Archive): 156

Leslie Schwab for HAER: 40, 68T, 70, 113, 121, 181L

Gretchen Van Dusen for HAER: vii

Raphael Villalobos for HAER: vii

Construction of the Siuslaw River Bridge, 1935

Index

Page locators in *italics* indicate photographs and diagrams. Entries in **bold typeface** indicate bridges designed by Conde B. McCullough.

Colophon

Oregon Coast Bridges is printed on 100# Inspire Earth dull book stock. The cover incorporates a color-build process black design with process color text highlights printed onto coated one-side 100# Inspire Earth dull cover. Titles, display headings, and main body text are set in Adobe Garamond Pro, a contemporary typeface family of Adobe Corporation, based on the roman types of Claude Garamond and the italic types of Robert Granjon. The layout was created using Adobe InDesign on the Windows 7 platform.

The Historic American Engineering Record/National Park Service photographs were made with a Cambo 45 NX camera and edited in Adobe Photoshop. Additional photos were prepared as 30MB, 8-bit TIFF files from a Nikon D2x digital SLR and Nikon 12-24 mm DX. Supplementary digital photos were taken with a 4 megapixel camera. Publication was output to PDF and submitted electronically to printer.

Oregon Coast Bridges was produced by James Norman. Mark A. Falby created the book design, cover and layout, provided photo enhancement/restoration services and graphics/illustrations creation. The book was printed by Bridgetown Printing Co. in Portland, Oregon. The softbound edition was bound by Portland Bindery. Signatures for the casebound edition were smythe-sewn and bound by Roswell Book Binding.